A Practical Guide to

# Data Base
# Management

# AUERBACH Data Processing Management Library

## James Hannan, Editor

•

### Contributors To This Volume

**Grayce Booth**
Honeywell Information Systems, Phoenix AZ

———

**Martin E. Modell**
Systems Architect, Merrill Lynch, New York NY

———

**T. William Olle**
Consultant, Surrey, England

———

**Bernard K. Plagman**
The PLAGMAN Group, New York NY

———

**Myles E. Walsh**
Director of Information Systems Planning, CBS, New York NY

———

**Jay-Louise Weldon**
Graduate School of Business Administration, New York University, New York NY

———

**J. Chris Wood**
Datacrown Incorporated, Arlington VA

———

**John W. Young, Jr.**
Systems Engineering, NCR Corporation, Scripps Ranch, San Diego CA

———

A Practical Guide to

# Data Base
# Management

Edited by James Hannan

AUERBACH Publishers Incorporated
Pennsauken NJ

VAN NOSTRAND REINHOLD COMPANY
New York  Cincinnati  Toronto  London  Melbourne

QA
76
.9
.D3
P725
1982
c.1

Library of Congress Catalog Card Number 82-11340

ISBN 0-442-20916-9

Printed in the United States of America

Published in the United States in 1982
by Van Nostrand Reinhold Company Inc
135 West 50th Street
New York NY 10020 USA

16 15 14 13 12 11 10 9 8 7 6 5 4 3 2 1

Library of Congress Cataloging in Publication Data
Main entry under title:

A Practical guide to data base management.

(Auerbach data processing management library ; v. 4)
1. Data base management. I. Hannan, James,
1946-      . II. Series.
QA76.9.D3P725   1982      658'.054      82-11340
ISBN 0-442-20916-9 (Van Nostrand Reinhold Co. : pbk.)

# Contents

# Preface

In its relatively brief existence, the computer has emerged from the back rooms of most organizations to become an integral part of business life. Increasingly sophisticated data processing systems are being used today to solve increasingly complex business problems. As a result, the typical data processing function has become as intricate and specialized as the business enterprise it serves.

Such specialization places a strenuous burden on computer professionals. Not only must they possess specific technical expertise, they must understand how to apply their special knowledge in support of business objectives and goals. A computer professional's effectiveness and career hinge on how ably he or she manages this challenge.

To assist computer professionals in meeting this challenge, AUERBACH Publishers has developed the *AUERBACH Data Processing Management Library*. The series comprises eight volumes, each addressing the management of a specific DP function:

A Practical Guide to Data Processing Management
A Practical Guide to Programming Management
A Practical Guide to Data Communications Management
A Practical Guide to Data Base Management
A Practical Guide to Systems Development Management
A Practical Guide to Data Center Operations Management
A Practical Guide to EDP Auditing
A Practical Guide to Distributed Processing Management

Each volume contains well-tested, practical solutions to the most common and pressing set of problems facing the manager of that function. Supplying the solutions is a prominent group of DP practitioners—people who make their living in the areas they write about. The concise, focused chapters are designed to help the reader directly apply the solutions they contain to his or her environment.

AUERBACH has been serving the information needs of computer professionals for more than 25 years and knows how to help them increase their effectiveness and enhance their careers. The *AUERBACH Data Processing Management Library* is just one of the company's many offerings in this field.

James Hannan
Assistant Vice President
AUERBACH Publishers

# Introduction

An increasing number of organizations have come to view the computerized data used in their operations as a valuable asset. This viewpoint has led to greater demands on DP professionals to manage their organizations' data more efficiently and effectively, spawning the concept of data resource management. In their attempts to meet those demands, many DP professionals have turned to data base technology.

Data base, as both a concept and a set of technologies, has been in existence for more than two decades. The data base approach to information systems evolved, in large measure, in response to the problems associated with what can be termed the "applications-centered approach." With the latter, separate data files are built for different applications; each application defines its own data elements together with their relationships and storage structures. The collection of these discrete, independent applications is considered an organization's "information system." The problems with such a system are obvious: data redundancy, processing and storage inefficiencies, excessive program maintenance, and questionable data consistency, integrity, and reliability.

In contrast, the data base approach stresses minimal data redundancy, faster processing times, reduced storage requirements, program independence from changes in the storage structure or logical views of data, and central administration and definition of data. Achieving these goals, however, is no simple matter.

Adopting the data base approach requires not only a sizable investment in expensive technology, but a fundamental change in information management practices. Without such a change, even the best data base management system (DBMS) can become little more than a sophisticated access device. This volume of the *AUERBACH Data Processing Management Library* is designed to help those charged with planning, implementing, and maintaining a data base environment make cost-effective decisions regarding the available technological tools and management techniques that comprise the data base approach.

We have commissioned an outstanding group of data base practitioners to share the benefits of their extensive and varied experience. Our authors have written on a carefully chosen range of topics and have provided proven, practical advice for managing the data base function productively.

In Chapter One, Martin E. Modell discusses the formidable management issues that must be resolved in establishing a data base environment and provides a strategy for careful planning and coordination of a data base project.

An important planning issue is convincing upper management to approve a data base project—they must be provided with reliable information and apprised of the specific benefits to be achieved. In his "Justifying a Data Base System," John W. Young, Jr., discusses the reasons for initiating a data base project and provides a practical and systematic method for justifying the data base approach to management.

Selecting and installing a DBMS also requires careful planning; both managerial and technical problems will likely be encountered. T. William Olle describes and analyzes many of these problems and offers practical advice on how to avoid them in Chapter Three.

Designing a data base and developing systems in a data base environment are complex undertakings. The factors involved in data base design are numerous and interrelated. Attempting to consider all their relationships can enmesh the designer in seemingly endless analysis. To aid the data base designer, Jay-Louise Weldon describes the methods for recognizing and evaluating the trade-offs inherent in data base design in Chapter Four. In Chapter Five, Bernard K. Plagman highlights the problems that systems developers are likely to encounter in a data base environment and describes ways for solving them.

Data sharing is a key component—and a major benefit—of a data base environment. Unfortunately, it is often very difficult to convince users to share "their" data. Understandably, users will agree to share data only if their requirements for acceptable downtime and system throughput are met. Thus effectively dealing with such crucial issues as restart/recovery and concurrency is vital to the success of the data base approach in any organization. J. Chris Wood addresses the former issue in his "Restart and Recovery in DBMSs" and discusses how to design effective restart and recovery mechanisms. John Young treats the latter issue in Chapter Seven and proposes a workable solution to concurrency—a locking mechanism that minimizes the possibility of deadlock.

Distributed data base environments pose a unique set of managerial and technical problems. Administrative control of data in such an environment is mandatory. The traditional role of the data/data base administrator, however, is patterned for a centralized environment. Thus new strategies for administration and control must be developed. In Chapter Eight, Bernard Plagman examines alternative strategies and offers practical guidelines that can be followed in this area.

The problems associated with administering and controlling data in a distributed environment are compounded when the data resides on unlike computers. Grayce Booth discusses these problems and suggests program and data migration as methods of solving them in Chapter Nine.

# Introduction

The old saw, "Experience is the best teacher," is well illustrated in Myles E. Walsh's description of a successful IMS/VS implementation. In Chapter Ten, Walsh describes the background of the project, the project teams, the sequence of project events, training, and the lessons his organization learned.

# 1 Data Base: A Management Perspective

by Martin E. Modell

## INTRODUCTION

The compilation of transactions generated as a result of doing business results in information. In a sense, this information can be called a data base. A company data base, in its broadest sense, consists of all information, or data, that comprises the records of the firm.

Organizations are slowly realizing that data is one of their most valuable resources; in fact, some companies today would go out of business if they lost access to their data files. These same companies are also recognizing that rapid access to timely, accurate data enables them to grow and prosper as never before.

Some companies, however, find themselves in a precarious position. They have acquired the technological tools to manage their data, with the intention of using that technology to create corporate data bases. They have not, however, come to grips with the problems of tailoring their systems, much less their organizations, to reflect the thinking that must accompany the establishment of a data base environment. In addition, they have not adequately defined their concept of data base, nor have they recognized that such definition is necessary. Neither have they adequately defined the parameters of a data base environment; moreover, there is still confusion about the terminology of technological implementation.

The use of integrated file structures, in which users share common data, implies centralized control, which, in turn, can cause many organizational problems. The question of data ownership is one of these problems. There is a function that originates data, a function that maintains it, a function that relies on it for daily operations, and a function that determines its termination. These functions may reside in many corporate areas. Who may authorize access to this data? Who may authorize change or modification? Who actually owns the data?

This chapter addresses the new organizational relationships, requirements, and management approach that should be developed when establishing a data base environment. It examines the design criteria for a data base environment from a management viewpoint and delineates the considerations involved in evaluating data base alternatives. A rationale for the analysis that leads to the objective determination of data structures and, therefore, data base requirements within an organization is presented, as is a discussion of data base-related cost considerations.

## DATA AS A RESOURCE—TECHNOLOGY VERSUS METHODOLOGY

The value of data is assessed by the extent to which it can be retrieved, processed, and presented to aid a particular decision or action. Data has no value if it cannot be located or processed in time. The value of data also depends on the accuracy and precision of its definition and the acceptability of that definition to the recipient.

Information within an organization is analogous to a river—it flows from point to point with little effective control or standardization, and its boundaries are ill defined. Thus, its accuracy is usually suspect, and its usefulness is severely diminished.

There is a growing realization that data, or information, is a business resource and must be managed as such. Because traditional techniques for resource management only partially address this task, new methodologies must be developed.

What makes this concern both unique and difficult is that all other resources have a logical place of control and residence within an organization. Information and data, however, pervade the organization, and they are generally inaccurately identified, ill defined, and ill controlled at the organizational level. The challenge in harnessing these resources is not so much a technological issue as it is a question of methodology. The technology of data base is not new; but the methodology of data resource management is.

### The Rationale for Creating a Data Base

With the growth of computer capacity and speed, we can now process information rapidly and consistently. We also have the technical tools and facilities to control, manage, and present information. The methodologies and techniques of design, the designs themselves, and the processing, however, still only replicate the manual processes they have supplanted. Thus, we are coupling primitive methodology and advanced technology in order to process information. We still process raw, unorganized data to produce information with marginal or narrow usefulness.

Organizations need to record data for both short- and long-term use. The systematic, short-term, accurate recording of data is basic to the successful daily operation and long-term survival of the organization. By providing a permanent record of the corporation's activities, the archiving of data sustains the auditing, statistical, forecasting, and control functions.

Usually, information is stored in a decentralized manner, which reflects the functional departmentalization of the organization. Payroll records, for instance, are usually stored in the payroll or accounting department, personnel records in the personnel department.

Some records, however, are stored in more than one functional area. Copies of purchase orders, for example, might be kept in purchasing, inventory, receiving, quality control, accounting, and in the originating department itself. As each area performs its part of the processing, the base information is modified. Rarely, if ever, are all copies of the base information changed in unison; thus, to gain a complete picture of a particular transaction, one must look into the files of each area that had access to or processed the purchase order in some way.

As a result (and to the detriment of the firm), the information in each processing area is incomplete or, worse, inaccurate. At best, it is suspect. In any case, only those areas that have copies can use the information. Thus, the view management has of information it receives is biased toward the area from which it was obtained (i.e., only information germane to a given area can be expected from that area).

## RELATION OF DATA BASE TO MIS

The term information has been used to designate data arranged in an ordered and useful form. Thus, management information can be thought of as information acquired as a result of business operations and presented to management in order to achieve specific purposes or enhance understanding.

The theoretical aim of a management information system (MIS) is to create an integrated series of systems (one for each major organizational function) to provide management with the information it needs, how and when it needs it. The greatest problem in the creation of a management information system arises from the traditional, functional approach to data. Usually, no single file of information is sufficient to answer more than simple queries. Answering complex questions requires going to multiple files, extracting information, and creating another file, which then must be processed in the required manner.

**Corporate Information System.** A corporate information system implies that while individual functional areas may have their separate systems, for corporate purposes there must be a certain level of aggregation and integration that allows upper management to view the corporate functional system from an organizational level. Thus, the unifying thread of a corporate information system is not the fact that it is a single system serving all but rather that the data, which acts as the base for all parts, is common to all who need information. The integration is really a consolidation of all like elements of data (i.e., those related to the same subject [although not necessarily real-world] entries). An organization with files of purchase orders; invoices; payments; and inventory, receiving, and vendor information, for example, could consolidate them into a material management data base in which all data related to that integrated function would reside as an integrated whole, with data segregated and organized against a logical model reflecting the natural aggregates of data and the relationships that exist among them. Thus, management information systems can be transformed into corporate information systems founded on the data base approach (see Figure 1-1).

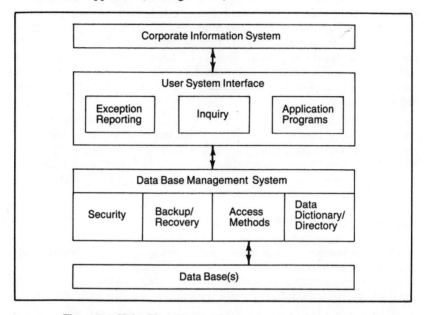

Figure 1-1. Major Elements of a Corporate Information System

## Multiple Management Levels

All managers need an understanding of the purpose of their organization (i.e., its policies, programs, plans, and goals). Individual managers differ, however, in their other informational requirements, the ways in which they have to view information, their analytical approaches in using it, and their conceptual organization of relevant facts.

An additional factor that complicates the management of information is the organizational level of the individual manager (see Figure 1-2). A manager at a lower operating level needs information to help him make daily operating decisions. At the upper levels, however, information is needed to support long-range planning and policy decisions. Managers at the various organizational levels also require different degrees of information summarization. In addition, they must be able to probe the corporate data base in order to obtain answers to questions, especially those that are vague or poorly defined when first asked. The success of corporate information systems thus depends on methodologies that produce:

- A common data base (or base of data)
- A common and consistent definition of the components of that data base that is accepted throughout the organization
- A data organization flexible enough to support structured or unstructured queries

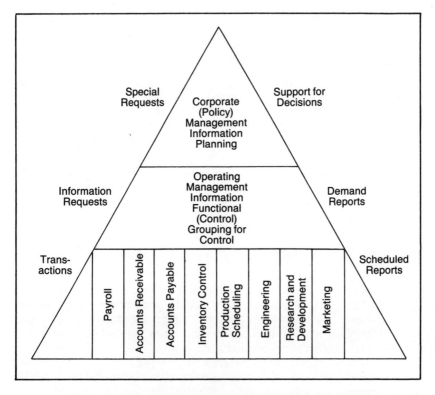

**Figure 1-2. Levels of Information Required in an Organization**

## Data Base

Traditionally, DP support activities have been oriented toward single departments and functional operational applications. In most cases, information is defined and organized differently for each application; thus, the data is often expensively duplicated (with an increase in the possibility of error) and impossible to integrate in meaningful ways. Information from payroll and personnel files, for example, could be combined only with great difficulty because of the different methods of classifying or identifying employees. Better integration of information-producing activities should lead to information that is more complete and relevant. The corporate move toward a data base environment must attempt to achieve this.

Input data, for example, must be commonly defined and consistently organized. Transactions must be set up so that they can be entered into the system once and can update all of the requisite data base records. In addition, such data as part numbers and customer and employee identification codes must be standardized. This approach eliminates duplicate data storage and also introduces integration and integrity.

Because many organizational units would be able to use such a common data resource, a centralized function is required to manage and protect it. Each unit cannot be allowed to modify data at will. Access to, and the processing of, the data base must be controlled.

The management of data is analogous to the management of finances. Just as there is a controller to manage money, there must be an administrator to manage data. Just as the controller uses ledgers, balance sheets, statements, and journals to record and control financial items, the data administrator uses function logical designs, libraries, documentation, and dictionaries to control and structure data items.

Each element of data has a source, an owner, and at least one use. The data administrator can use the aforementioned tools to describe them. He can also employ data base management systems to store data and to provide access and security.

## Data Base Administration

The data administration function must deal with the following questions:
- Most information systems today serve the needs of operating supervisors and, to a lesser extent, middle managers, with little or no direct support provided to upper management. How can data bases be structured to satisfy the information needs of all levels of management? Is it possible to organize and structure a single set of data bases to meet the needs at each level, or must different data bases be created for different horizontal levels?
- Can different functional areas share a data base? Can a single data base supply the information needed by managers at different levels with diverse functions, or must separate, vertical data bases be designed for each gross function? Should an attempt be made to integrate functionally separate data requirements into one data base that will serve the broader needs of a cross-function environment?
- Managers at the higher levels need information about the external world. The quality of externally produced data, however, is more difficult to control than internal data quality since the definition is less precise; moreover, external data is expensive to obtain. Should data from external sources be incorporated into the data base(s)? Can we ensure that this information is complete, timely, and accurate?
- Different managers occupying the same position over a period of time will have different informational needs, and the system should not have to be redesigned to meet these changing requirements. Can suitable flexibility be built into the logical data structures that underlie the data base(s)?

To address these and other questions, we must define the various forms a data base can assume and the components that must be developed, either for many different data bases, each one serving a particular functional unit (i.e., decentralized data bases) or for one data base serving all parts of the organization (i.e., a centralized data base). In this context, the impact of each of these forms on the organization must be evaluated.

This evaluation should not be performed from the perspective of the software that makes data base implementation possible. It should not deal with the hardware and personnel problems inherent in a data base environment. Rather, the methodology for evaluation should focus on:

- Defining the data base requirements
- Designing the structure
- Specifying the degree of sharing that will occur
- Protecting the data base(s)

This evaluation should be augmented with an analysis of the required decision-support framework and the effect that the data base discipline will have on the organization's operations. In addition, the data administration function should be clearly defined.

## COST IMPLICATIONS

Another management consideration is the cost of data base implementation. This is especially so because the cost of a data base program can differ considerably from other DP costs. The payoff period from the data base program is longer than that derived from increasing the hardware configuration or adding programmers. Because DP has grown so rapidly, managers are accustomed to change; however, in the past, change occurred in direct response to a strong user demand. This is not the case in the data base environment. The manager must fully appreciate the cost behavior of the data base program and make a concerted effort to control costs.

**Out-of-Pocket Costs.** Since out-of-pocket costs have an immediate impact on the operating budgets, the high cost of the data base effort is of great concern to the line manager. The high cost includes the price of software, hardware, and programmers and extends to the labor costs of developing standards and procedures and coordinating numerous requirements.

**Misuse of Data Base Software.** Another type of cost that may be incurred is that resulting from misuse of data base software. In order to compromise between going to a full-fledged data base system and maintaining the user's custom system, nonstandard use of data base software may be implemented. A situation can therefore result in which semi-integrated files are processed using data base software. This becomes a costly compromise when expensive maintenance problems, poor system integration, and inefficient use of software result.

**Hidden Costs.** Managers who commit to data base technology must realize that many hidden costs exist. Since the data base can change the basic way in which systems work, many costs are not readily discernible until the actual changes are made. Although managers cannot be relieved of their responsibility for thoroughness, the following costs are not obvious:

- The relationship between software and hardware (because new software may require additional core or hardware).
- Software changes requiring unanticipated hardware upgrades to maintain improvements or realize performance.
- User need to commit large blocks of time to integrate previously independent systems. (The delays that can be caused in this situation are costly.)
- The cost of running parallel systems (especially disk and labor costs).
- The task of keeping up with the latest software releases to realize the benefits of new capabilities.
- The need for specific documentation and procedures.
- An initial increase in applications design time because of the learning curve and the requirement for more coordination.

**Data Resource Accounting System.** Giving data the status of a corporate resource has important ramifications in terms of accounting. Most management control and accounting systems do not provide a good mechanism for apprising management of its data costs; therefore, the need for a data resource accounting system is evident. Most firms treat the costs of creating data or a data base as an expense and do not attempt to give the product an asset value. To many firms, data is a more important asset than the physical plant; yet this fact is not reflected on the books. Data, as a resource and asset, has many attributes that should be captured in the accounting practice for tax purposes and should be used to reflect the true market value of the organization.

## CONCLUSION

In preparing for a data base environment, management should focus on the issues described in this chapter and emphasize the management of data as a resource. The formation of an organizational unit to address data administration issues is an important step in this direction.

**Bibliography**

Davis, Gordon B. *Management Information Systems.* New York: McGraw-Hill Book Company, 1974.

Sanders, Donald H. *Computers and Management in a Changing Society,* 2nd ed. New York: McGraw-Hill Book Company, 1974.

"Selection and Acquisition of Data Base Management Systems." A report of the CODASYL Systems Committee, 1976.

Sibley, Edgar H. "The Development of Data Base Technology." *Computing Surveys,* Vol. 8, No. 2 (March 1976).

# 2 Justifying a Data Base System

by John W. Young, Jr.

## INTRODUCTION

Justifying a data base system to management is a precarious process. Because data base is a relatively new concept in the DP industry, many organizations are switching to a data base approach, with little or no understanding of the concept. What is worse, management is often asked to decide on a data base project on the basis of incorrect or insufficient information or false justifications. If management is provided with the wrong information, it is likely to reject the project. On the other hand, false justification may convince management to approve a data base project that will only be abandoned when it fails to produce the promised results. It is vital, therefore, to the success of a data base project (and, consequently, to the welfare of the organization) that the data base system be carefully designed to meet user needs and that the real benefits to be gained from its implementation be fully and correctly presented to management.

A data base system represents a philosophy of organizing data into an integrated whole to meet the following objectives:
* Protect the integrity of the data
* Make all data easily available to whichever users and programs need it, both for one-time requests and for new application systems
* Minimize unnecessary data redundancy
* Bring the data under the unified control of a DBMS in order to meet the first three objectives

This chapter discusses the data base system approach but does not discuss specific data base management systems.

## FAVORABLE ENVIRONMENT FOR A DATA BASE SYSTEM

A frequent end-user complaint is that the DP department is incapable of meeting their informational needs. Users often complain that reports are wrong or do not reflect current information. In addition, it is often difficult or too time-consuming to get a new report when needed. A brief exploration of these complaints helps explain the friction between users and the DP department.

**Reports Are Wrong.** The many reasons why reports are often wrong range from the mundane (e.g., an error during initial data entry) to the exotic (e.g., an incorrect program flow is produced by an unanticipated and unprecedented set of data values or conditions). In fact, these two types of errors constitute a large percentage of the errors in single-file applications.

Another major source of error involves programs that read several files at the same time. Resulting report errors occur because of a lack of file synchronization. This problem can be illustrated with the following example.

A bank maintains a file of savings customers and a file of checking customers. A report is to be prepared listing all customers who have both kinds of accounts; the files are to be matched based on customer name and address. If the savings file is updated on second shift and the checking file on third shift, a problem can occur: if a change of address received for a customer is to be applied to both files that night and the match report is run at the end of the second shift (i.e., before the checking file is updated), that customer's addresses will not match, and the report will be incorrect. This problem is further (and perhaps permanently) compounded if the customer gives the new address as "517 North Pennsylvania St" on one change form and "517 N. Penn" on the other. Only a very sophisticated matching program can detect the fact that these addresses are really the same.

**Reports Do Not Reflect Current Information.** If information is maintained in a collection of separate files, the time lag in updating them can result in reports not bearing current information. Thus, in an online order entry system in which several files contain stock levels and orders and queries arrive continuously, timely reports can be achieved only if much effort is devoted to synchronization.

**Reports Are Too Hard to Get.** To improve their decision making, management constantly demands more and better-organized information. Because these demands are often unpredictable, however, providing this kind of information can be a major source of frustration to management and the DP department alike. In addition, producing the desired reports often involves assembling and processing information from various sources within the total body of information available to the organization, and developing programs that use multiple files is a difficult job. There are several complicating factors:
- One or more of the files may lack proper documentation (e.g., certain fields may no longer exist although the most recent record layouts show that they do, or there may be dummy records with check totals that are known only to the programmer who put them there).
- The files may be sorted on different keys.
- The owner of one of the files may not wish to surrender it, thus setting off a series of management clashes.

These factors, plus the laboriousness of working with relatively low-level programming languages, often mean that the need for a particular report will have passed before it can be prepared; or a manager may be informed that the requested information is unavailable even though the basic data elements required to produce it exist in machine-readable form [1].

## Symptoms of File-Related Problems

The problems that prompt the preceding complaints can manifest themselves in many ways. Typical symptoms of these problems include:
- A large backlog of unfilled requests to the DP department.
- Managers attempting to manually combine the data from several reports. (This is often an indication of the DP department's inability to combine information from several files in a single report.)
- Taking an excessive amount of time to close the books each month. In the competitive business world, it is unrealistic and unreasonable to require a manager to make month-end decisions before month-end data is available.

## UNFAVORABLE ENVIRONMENT FOR A DATA BASE SYSTEM

There are certain environments in which a data base system might be inappropriate. Although certain conditions may not entirely preclude consideration of a data base system, the environment must be examined carefully to ensure that it is well suited to a transition to data base.

## Satisfied Users

The purpose of a data base system is to provide more accurate and timely information to the user community. If the community is satisfied with the present information system, it would be presumptuous to attempt to justify changes or additions to the system. It should be carefully verified, however, that the users are really satisfied with the system and are not just adopting an attitude of "Oh, what's the use of asking for anything else; we'll never get it anyway!"

## Recently Introduced File Systems

The chief benefit of a data base system results from replacing a heterogeneous collection of files with an integrated data base. If there have been recent, substantial investments in the development of file-oriented systems, however, it may be difficult to cost justify moving to a data base approach.

## Lack of Proper Organizational Environment

Data base systems are a revolutionary departure from the traditional file-oriented approach to data handling. The transition to a data base environment can be hindered by several organizational factors [2].

**No Continuity of Organizational Policy.** The objectives of the organization must be stable, since the purpose of the data base approach is to help fulfill those objectives. It should be noted, however, that once the system is installed, it can help cope with moderately changing goals.

**High Personnel Turnover.** Employees must be trained in the design and use of systems in the data base environment. Conducting this training when there is constant staff turnover is a very difficult task.

**Management Resistance to New Ideas.** Changing to a data base environment introduces new DP concepts and techniques but also shifts the relationships between the DP organization and the users. Management at all levels must be prepared to accept the organizational and procedural changes that are required in this new environment—an environment in which data is viewed as a corporate asset as significant as inventory or buildings.

## Lack of Technical Foundation

Data base management systems are intended to handle a variety of complex batch and online requirements and to provide satisfactory throughput and response times. Designing the logical and physical structure of the data base and properly interfacing programs to the data base usually require a moderate to high degree of specialized knowledge and technical skill. Although this skill may not be currently available in the DP organization, the personnel who are to work with the data base must quickly acquire the necessary in-depth technical expertise through self-study, courses and seminars, and vendor training.

Inadequacies in this area quickly become apparent when an application runs several times more slowly in the data base environment than it did using conventional files. If such a situation arises, it may be necessary to seek expert advice from a consultant or vendor representative. Such help may also be necessary to fill in gaps in employees' technical training (e.g., to indicate design errors and to show how to avoid similar errors in the future).

The lack of appropriate or adequate technical background can result in wasteful use of computer resources, poor response to user needs, and, worst of all, a data base whose contents may or may not be correct. Such factors can jeopardize the whole data base project. It is important to avoid these pitfalls by ensuring that the installation has people capable of being trained as well as the resources available to prepare them for their new responsibilities.

## Lack of Data Base Administration

Administration of the data base resource by a single centralized group is essential to the effectiveness of the data base approach. This does not mean that the needs or wishes of individual managers are ignored but, rather, that the data base administration staff controls the development of the system and ensures that a coordinated structure is planned from the beginning. Failure to establish this group and to provide it with adequate authority to carry out its function can result in a patchwork of system fragments instead of a smoothly functioning integrated data base.

## JUSTIFYING A DATA BASE MANAGEMENT SYSTEM

The arguments for justifying a data base management system (DBMS) to management must be carefully formulated. The acquisition and installation of a DBMS represents a substantial investment and is likely to be undertaken only if equally substantial potential benefits can be documented. Fortunately, those benefits are often evident, and the DP department almost always has the support of the users in presenting them. When possible, the benefits should be quantified so that actual financial savings can be shown.

The principal justifications for a DBMS are described in the following sections.

### Increased Data Integrity

**Correctness.** Since a given data element exists at only one place in a data base, there is no possibility of inconsistent versions of an element. The value of this can be described in terms of the consequences, possibly financial, of incorrect or inconsistent data use in critical operations. It should also be pointed out, if true, that validation criteria are applied to prevent incorrect data from entering the data base.

**Security.** DBMSs usually have some security mechanism to prevent unauthorized access to data. This facility keeps sensitive personal or corporate data from being compromised and thus avoids consequent financial liability or loss of competitive advantage.

**Protection and Recovery.** It has been pointed out that data is an important corporate resource that merits the same degree of protection as any other property. Each system user must be assured that once their data has been entrusted to the data base system, it will be safe from damage. Just as guards protect physical property, the DBMS safeguards the data. System cost can be measured against the consequences to the organization if portions of its operational information (e.g., accounts receivable) are lost.

### Better Response to User Needs

**Special Reports.** The users' need to quickly obtain organized and formatted special reports from existing data is undoubtedly a major factor in deciding to install a DBMS. The value of this DBMS capability can be measured against two criteria:
- The cost to the organization of not having the desired information available
- The cost to assemble the information manually or in some other fashion without the DBMS

**New Applications.** Users are continually expanding their horizons in terms of what new applications can be introduced profitably. DBMSs hasten the development of new applications in two ways. Since the data and its description is centralized, it is easier to plan new applications; that is, information about scattered and uncoordinated files does not have to be assembled from multiple sources of perhaps questionable accuracy. In addition, DBMSs provide tools for faster and more accurate programming of new applications. Thus, programmers can usually devote more effort to the functioning of the system and less to the details of record storage, access, and processing. This faster development is reflected in three benefits that can be presented as part of DBMS justification:

- Less effort is required on the part of system analysts and programmers, resulting in a saving in personnel costs.
- The benefits of new applications are realized sooner; thus, return on investment starts earlier.
- A shorter development cycle provides less chance for changing application requirements; thus, the development process is simplified.

## Improved Usability of Data

**Improved Timeliness.** The fact that data in a data base is easier to keep updated results in several advantages. First, decisions are made on the basis of the latest information. In presenting this justification, examples should be submitted of cases in which rapidly changing conditions made it essential for management to have the very latest data—cases in which there would have been a financial penalty if the most recent data was unavailable. Second, the organization can directly achieve a monetary gain through faster information processing (e.g., bills can be sent out in 5 days instead of 15). The increased value of the funds being available sooner can be calculated and presented.

**More Flexible Data Structures.** A characteristic of DBMSs is that they allow for more flexible associations among data elements. Although this advantage is difficult to quantify, it clearly results in both easier system design and in a better fit between user needs and system output.

**Less Redundancy.** Data storage is now sufficiently inexpensive that the nonredundancy offered by the data base approach may not be a major benefit. The improved consistency of data, however, as well as the savings in not having to update multiple copies of the same information should be considered for presentation as part of DBMS justification.

## Easier Adaptation to Future Change

**Data Independence.** A major advantage of the data base approach is that it largely insulates application programs from the effects of changes in logical data structures or in physical data organization, hardware, or media. If such changes can be projected for the future, savings in analysis, programming, and program recompilation and testing can be claimed.

**Distributed Data Processing.** The centralized control and knowledge inherent in a data base can make a transition to distributed DP much easier. This justification is usually purely qualitative.

## False Expectations

There are, however, two areas in which it might be thought that a data base could reduce the requirements for DP resources but in which savings are seldom achieved: staff size and computer resources. It is widely believed that a smaller DP staff would be required with a data base system. This is almost certainly false for the first year of development. It usually requires two to three years to begin realizing savings in personnel. By that time, additional requirements have appeared, necessitating additional staff members.

If an organization has much redundant data that is being synchronized and maintained, there is a chance that a data base system would slightly reduce computer resource utilization. In general, however, DBMSs require more computer resources because they are generalized and are designed to satisfy a wide range of requirements.

## ESTIMATING THE COST OF A DATA BASE SYSTEM

Although some of the benefits of data base implementation are difficult to quantify, estimating the associated cost is a relatively straightforward process. Since the cost is totally dependent on the nature and size of the organization and on the scope of the proposed data base environment, no attempt is made in this chapter to present absolute times or costs of these efforts. It should be noted, however, that part of the justification process is to carefully estimate the cost of each task and its duration. This can be done by deciding how many users would have to be interviewed, how long each interview would take, how much work would be involved in writing up the interview results, and so on.

In the following paragraphs, a typical data base project has been divided into a number of major tasks that should be considered when determining the cost of data base implementation. Table 2-1, which identifies the major cost items associated with each task, can serve as a checklist of cost items in each category.

**Feasibility Study.** This study presents the current state of an information system in order to decide whether it is worthwhile to further investigate the possible installation of a data base system.

**User Survey and Information Flow.** A comprehensive examination of the information requirements of an organization, this phase of the effort is by far the most exacting and time-consuming. It consists of interviewing potential users of a data base system as well as covering the organization's existing data flows and processing. Future needs must also be included, taking into account

**Table 2-1. Major Expense Items**

| Major Expense Category | Expense Items | Approximate Cost $ |
|---|---|---|
| Feasibility Study | Education of technical staff | _____ |
| | Analyst time | _____ |
| | Consultants fees | _____ |
| User Survey and | Interviewer time | _____ |
| Information Flow Analysis | Interviewee time | _____ |
| | DBA staff time | _____ |
| | Project manager time | _____ |
| | Analyst time | _____ |
| | Application programmer time | _____ |
| | Clerical support time | _____ |
| Data Analysis | DBA design staff time | _____ |
| | Consultants fees | _____ |
| Data Dictionary | Software package cost | _____ |
| | Clerical support and data entry time | _____ |
| Cost/Benefit Analysis | Research time | _____ |
| | Report preparation time | _____ |
| Package Evaluation, | Education of technical staff | _____ |
| Selection, and Acquisition | DBA staff time | _____ |
| | Consultants fees | _____ |
| | Travel expense | _____ |
| | Benchmarking and evaluation cost | _____ |
| | Contract preparation, review, and negotiation time | _____ |
| | Initial package and maintenance costs | _____ |
| | Additional hardware and software costs | _____ |
| Initial System Design | Computer analyst time | _____ |
| | User time | _____ |
| | Vendor representative time | _____ |
| | Consultants fees | _____ |

possible new activities, improved decision making, and so on. The work needed to thoroughly document the results of the study must not be overlooked.

**Data Dictionary Installation.** Most of the input for this task comes from the information flow analysis and user survey. There is substantial data entry associated with this task; the magnitude of this undertaking depends on whether the data dictionary can use the same data definition input as the data base system itself or whether two separate descriptions must be prepared. A software package is usually required to maintain the data dictionary.

**Cost/Benefit Analysis.** It is a good idea to do the benefit half of this task concurrently with the user survey. When a user mentions a particular data base service, the interviewer should request an estimate of the value of such a service (i.e., what the interviewee would be willing to pay for it).

**Data Analysis.** This is a study of the interrelationships among data entities in an organization. Such a study requires careful attention to detail; review by an external source (e.g., a consultant) may also be required.

**Package Evaluation, Selection, and Acquisition.** Selecting the most suitable data base package is a time-consuming and expensive process. It is important, therefore, that the evaluation criteria be chosen carefully to ensure appropriateness. Once selected, each criterion should be assigned a numerical weight that roughly approximates its perceived value. This facilitates comparison of the value of each criterion relative to the value of any other criterion. It also provides a simple method of assigning a single relative score to each package under consideration. The weighting scheme can be supplemented by preparing one list of characteristics that any package must have to be considered and another list of those attributes that it must not possess.

It is important not to skimp in the selection process. Although this process may be as costly as the package itself, the long-term costs and adverse consequences of choosing the wrong system make economizing in this area most unwise. Thus, although benchmarking can be expensive, it is sometimes recommended when deciding among several data base packages.

The costs involved in the actual acquisition of a DBMS (e.g., travel and contract preparation) should not be neglected. Naturally, the cost of the DBMS itself, maintenance fees, and the expense of any additional hardware and software required are of primary concern.

**Initial System Design.** The duration and cost of developing the initial application to use the DBMS depends on the application itself. In addition to the direct cost of the application are costs associated with training personnel in the system design techniques appropriate for the data base environment. It should be noted that if the first project fails, the entire data base effort will probably be scrapped; thus, it is usually advisable to procure outside help for the initial implementation.

## CONCLUSION

In a data base presentation for management, most costs and benefits are quantifiable. Quantifiable costs should be grouped in one section, nonquantifiable ones in another. A note of caution: an unsupportable dollar value assigned to a benefit may be vulnerable to attack by financial executives. Once one figure has been discredited, it is often assumed that all are suspect. Thus, much additional time might have to be spent in creating new justifications for every number in the cost/benefit analysis. All figures, therefore, should be carefully and realistically derived to minimize delay and to avoid embarrassment after the project has been approved.

**References**

1. Nolan, Richard. "Computer Data Base: The Future is Now." *Harvard Business Review* (September-October 1973).
2. CODASYL Systems Committee. *Selection and Acquisition of Data Base Management Systems.* Association for Computing Machinery, March 1976.

# ③ Pitfalls to Avoid in DBMS Implementation Planning

by T. William Olle

## INTRODUCTION

It is unfortunate that in the application of DP techniques during the past 20 years, many people have not learned from the mistakes of others. When an organization is planning for a DBMS, the potential benefits and risks are extremely high. It is essential, therefore, to be very careful and to consider all related aspects of a situation before making a decision.

DBMS implementation planning has a number of pitfalls that can be avoided. These include:
- Accepting a DBMS without careful evaluation
- Using the DBMS as a sophisticated access method
- Not recognizing the need to analyze application data
- Applying outdated information systems design methodologies
- A lack of management commitment
- Failure to recognize the intangible benefits
- Forgetting the data dictionary

In addition, several technical problems must be given careful attention. These pitfalls and problems are discussed in this chapter.

## TIMING THE DECISION

In a recent work, R.L. Nolan [1] states that organizations have a traditional learning curve to surmount as they absorb and attempt to profit from DP technology. Nolan's "stage hypothesis" identifies four stages of the learning curve:
- Stage 1—initiation
- Stage 2—contagion
- Stage 3—control
- Stage 4—integration

It is interesting to note that data base management starts to play a role in this learning curve in Stage 3—after the stage in which everyone has become enthusiastic and applications have proliferated. Nolan sees Stage 3 as the stage in which existing applications are consolidated; some applications may have to be rewritten in a consolidation of this type. Stage 4 is the stage in which the applications using the central data base are used in an online mode.

The point of this analysis is that all installations will sooner or later consider using a DBMS to consolidate applications and to obtain the benefits that can be achieved by integrating files into carefully designed and centrally controlled data bases.

Nevertheless, it is not always obvious *when* an installation should make the move into data base management, and it is even less obvious *how rapidly* it should proceed. There have been many sad tales of installations that made the move too early and too quickly and failed completely. Conversely, some installations proceeded so slowly that the result was disappointing.

Some organizations, however, have taken the bold step from a manual information system to a fully integrated data base approach. This is possible only when highly skilled personnel or consultants with related experience are available.

Making the move to a DBMS at the wrong time can be devastating. The problems with moving too early are related to the maturity of the data processing function in the organization, while moving too late can cause loss of a competitive edge in the marketplace.

## PROBLEMS PECULIAR TO ALL DBMSs

A number of DBMS-related problems can occur quite independently of the DBMS to be used. (This chapter borrows from a paper written by E.H. Sibley that was presented at the 1977 IFIP Congress in Toronto [2].)

### Technical Expertise Required

Assuming that the use of a DBMS requires no more expertise than does the use of conventional DP is analogous to taking a pilot out of a small, propeller-driven aircraft and putting him in charge of a commercial jetliner. The fact that he has flown a somewhat older kind of aircraft means only that he is a reasonable candidate for being trained to fly a jet. A similar argument can be applied to DP and DBMS personnel. Implementation of a DBMS lives or dies on the expertise available to do the job. Note that consultants can be contracted with and/or experienced personnel identified or recruited to ensure successful design and installation.

The change from conventional to data-base-oriented systems is difficult and should be treated with considerable care. A training program for all concerned must be established. Management-level personnel and end users require an orientation that does not present technical details but rather covers the essential differences between a conventional and a data base approach to building an information system. All technical personnel should receive thorough technical training. Frequent review meetings are also necessary to discuss problems encountered in design and development activities.

## Accepting a DBMS without Careful Evaluation

A number of fully developed DBMSs are currently available commercially. Users of IBM equipment are particularly fortunate because they can choose from more than five DBMSs, all of which have enjoyed from 6 to 10 years of useful (and, to a varying extent, productive) life. These DBMSs, however, vary considerably in technical characteristics; thus, a careful (six-month) comparative evaluation is essential.

In the early 1970s, there were not nearly as many DBMSs to choose from. A situation occurring frequently in Europe today is one in which a U.S. parent company who made its choice of DBMS in 1971 or 1972 now insists that its European subsidiary make the same choice. This can be unfortunate.

## Using the DBMS as a Sophisticated Access Method

It is sometimes tempting to use a DBMS as nothing more than an elaborate indexed sequential-access method. As such, a fairly simple application's magnetic file or existing ISAM file would be replaced by a fairly simple data base. This is an easy approach that may, in fact, offer some of the widely known advantages (e.g., better data independence) of using a DBMS. Doing this, however, is simply ignoring most of the potential DBMS advantages. The effect is rather like paying for a jet airliner and flying it at propeller-driven-aircraft speeds.

To obtain reasonable advantages from using a DBMS, one should select an initial application that requires between 15 and 20 record types. This will spur correct implementation of the DBMS and check any temptation to misuse the software.

## Not Recognizing the Need to Analyze Application Data

The need to analyze application data is now widely discussed by people experienced in the selection and application of DBMSs. The value of a data model (sometimes called a conceptual schema) as an indispensable aid to understanding the meaning of the data is now recognized. A data model should be designed first, and then the functions to be computerized should be analyzed and designed in terms of that data model.

It would be unfair to claim that there is a complete lack of controversy surrounding the idea of a data model. Although most people who have had experience with DBMSs recommend that some kind of data model be prepared, there is a difference of opinion between practitioners and theoreticians concerning the kind of data model that is most suitable. The essence of the controversy is the use of the concept of a record type that contains several data items. Theoreticians claim that grouping data items into a record type is making a storage decision that one might wish to modify after a period of use. The assertion is that better data independence can be achieved by developing a data model based on more fundamental constructs than the record type.

The cornerstone of the kind of data model advocated here is a data structure diagram (see Figure 3-1). This example shows a purchasing application in which tender, price quotations, and purchase orders can be requested. The diagram shows the static relationships between the various entities, each of which is illustrated in a rectangular box. The arrows between boxes show classic one-to-many relationships. Failure to perform the kind of analysis required to prepare a data model before selecting a DBMS is one of the most common and dangerous pitfalls that can be encountered in moving to a DBMS environment.

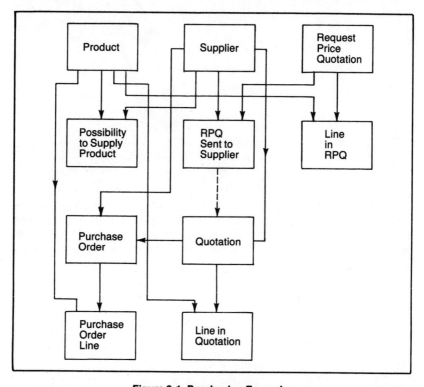

**Figure 3-1. Purchasing Example**

## Applying Outdated Information Systems Design Methodologies

Many useful design methodologies have emerged from conventional DP. Some of these techniques become part of an installation's design standard. Although it is good to have a systematic approach to design, the impact of data base design requirements on the information systems design methodology is often underestimated.

There are many design methodologies that rely on a basic INPUT-PROCESS-OUTPUT analysis. Such methodologies have a role to play in the design of application programs after a data base is designed. It is important, however, to avoid being too insistent about reconciling conventional information systems design methodology with data base design techniques.

## Lack of Management Commitment

It is tempting for managers to regard DBMS implementation (and, indeed, all problems connected with DP) as technical problems that they should not have to address. Unfortunately, the move to a DBMS cannot be ignored by management. If, for example, technical personnel choose to use the DBMS as an elaborate access method, management will probably not be affected by the changeover but will continue to experience frustration in its attempts to obtain integrated information overviews from the DP department. If the DBMS is to be correctly implemented, management's commitment must be a driving force.

## Failure to Recognize Intangible Benefits

After more than two decades of business experience with computers, it is understandable that management should seek cost justification for moving into a DBMS environment. All too often, management has approved the expenditure of funds only to be disappointed by the abortive or superficial nature of the results. The fact is that because many advantages of a data base environment are intangible, it is often difficult to produce two columns of figures that detail all associated costs and benefits. They become apparent only after several applications have been successfully implemented and integrated and are fully operational. At that point, it is quite possible that the systems will link across functional lines, providing unanticipated advantages to upper management.

## Forgetting the Data Dictionary

A data dictionary should be thought of as a special data base in which one stores data about the data in the main data base [3]. The term *meta-data-base* is sometimes used to describe this special kind of data base. When an organization has a large number of record types, data items, and programs, a data dictionary can be used as an administrative tool for controlling the record, item, and program names and showing how they are used in relation to each other.

It should be pointed out that a data dictionary is perfectly valid in the context of conventional application systems; however, with DBMSs, the mass of data about data is even more critical. This information should be stored in a data dictionary, which, by the way, can also conveniently store the results of the data analysis activity previously discussed.

## PROBLEMS PECULIAR TO SPECIFIC DBMSs

There are three problems that are peculiar to specific DBMSs; these problems may, however, be encountered with any DBMS to a greater or lesser degree.

## Restrictive Structuring Facilities

Each DBMS has certain restrictions in the way the designer can structure the data base. A restriction of this kind can be overcome simply by defining extra record types and extra relationships. This extra structure is often referred to as clutter. While a detailed discussion of this topic is outside the scope of this chapter, it is important to be aware of the problem because it can seriously influence the choice and operation of a DBMS. If a detailed DBMS selection study is performed in conjunction with an analysis of application data, the clutter that must be introduced into the data base design because of the shortcomings of a particular DBMS will become apparent and can be further evaluated.

## Hidden Execution-Time Overheads

DBMSs vary considerably in the efficiency of the generated code. Even if the data base is reasonably well defined within the confines of the structuring facilities, the user can still get a nasty shock when application program execution time is measured. This is particularly true for online systems in which terminal response time is so noticeable.

The difficulty with hidden execution-time overheads is basically this: the DBMS is designed so that it is easy for the applications programmers to write programs that are logically and functionally correct and will produce the desired result. This implies that the application programmer need not know what goes on behind the scenes. In fact, in order to write reasonably efficient code, the programmer does have to know what goes on behind the scenes. Consequently, an ease-of-use advantage may not exist. To circumvent this problem, careful analysis of DBMS structure and code is necessary. In addition, emphasis must be placed on training people to the level of expertise required to work the new system.

## Difficulty in Achieving the Desired Level of Data Independence

The possibility for achieving improved data independence is frequently cited as one of the prime reasons for using a DBMS.

Most systems must be extended after some period of use. This extension may involve designing and preparing new programs to process the existing data base. This does not usually create problems. The extensions may, however, require adding items to the existing data base. It may be necessary to add new items to existing record types, add completely new record types, or create new relationships between new and existing record types. If this can be done without affecting existing application programs, one can claim that the DBMS is supporting a reasonable level of data independence. With some commercially available DBMSs, however, it is simply not possible to add new data items to existing record types.

The solution is either to add extra record types and relationships, with the concomitant clutter and efficiency problems, or to undertake an extensive rewrite. Because this can be extremely expensive and cancels one of the prime reasons for using DBMS, it is most important to check data independence functions when performing the recommended DBMS comparative evaluation.

## CONCLUSION

The major pitfalls of DBMS implementation and use can be avoided through:

- The competence of the technical personnel and the involvement and commitment of management.
- Careful analysis of application data in order to understand the inherent complexities prior to embarking on an evaluation of DBMSs.
- Careful evaluation of available DBMSs and data dictionaries before committing the organization to a particular system.
- Choosing a pilot application system for the DBMS that is neither too small nor too large; suitable size is between 15 and 20 record types.

References

1. Nolan, R.L. "Thoughts about the Fifth Stage." *Data Base*, Vol. 7, No. 2 (Fall 1975), pp. 4–10.
2. Sibley, E.L. "The Impact of Data Base Technology on Business Systems." *Proceedings IFIP 77 Congress.* Toronto, Canada, 1977, pp.589–596.
3. Plagman, Bernard K. "Data Dictionary/Directory System—A Tool for Data Administration and Control." Portfolio 22-01-02. *AUERBACH Data Base Management*. Pennsauken NJ: AUERBACH Publishers Inc.

Bibliography

Gosline, W. George. "Data Independence in DBMS—Parts I and II." Portfolios 22-03-08 and 22-03-09. *AUERBACH Data Base Management*. Pennsauken NJ: AUERBACH Publishers Inc.

# ④ Trade-offs in Data Base Design

by Jay-Louise Weldon

## INTRODUCTION

In its broadest sense, data base design encompasses activities that range from the identification of end-user requirements to the final arrangement of data values on a physical device. The first phase of the design process, logical design [1], results in a formal description of the entities and relationships that must be captured by the data base to meet user requirements. The second phase, physical design [2], determines how the logical data base (the data base schema or data submodel [3]) should be physically represented for the most efficient data storage and processing. Many design decisions must be made during both phases; decisions made in one may affect the choices available in the other. The designer who errs in either phase or lacks knowledge of one phase's effect on the other can expect suboptimal results.

Many organizations are beginning to recognize the importance of the data base design process. Business organizations are increasingly moving from the traditional approach of developing data files that support specific applications to developing large, integrated data bases that can be shared by many users. In such an environment, design errors can be costly, not only to one application system but to any user accessing shared data. Design errors can also be costly in terms of excess or inefficient processing, excess device capacity, lengthy application development times, frequent data base reorganization, or required reprogramming of application programs.

Unfortunately, many organizations approach the data base design process with little or no understanding of the trade-offs. The designer must often make decisions based on intuition or experience with non-data-base systems. Design errors can be minimized, however, if the designer views the data base design process as a series of trade-offs.

A trade-off is the result of a knowledgeable assessment of the costs and benefits of a decision or action, in which one benefit is exchanged for another when the latter is deemed more desirable or of higher priority. Using trade-offs advantageously thus requires a knowledge of the effects of and interrelationships among factors involved in the decision.

Two classes of trade-offs can be identified for the process of data base design—general and operational. General trade-offs relate to the designer's approach to the overall design problem. They should serve as guidelines for selecting feasible alternatives for the logical and physical structure of the data base. Operational trade-offs [4], however, permit specific choices among design tools or among actual or proposed alternative data base structures. The designer should assess these trade-offs in terms of design alternatives and should use the results to select an implementation strategy that corresponds to organizational objectives.

## GENERAL TRADE-OFFS

The data base designer should be cognizant of the five general trade-offs that follow, which form the basis of a design philosophy that can guide the formulation of implementation alternatives. In addition, the designer can use these trade-offs to evaluate the general feasibility of different implementation approaches. Final decisions must, however, be made in conjunction with the evaluation of operational trade-offs.

**Specialization versus Generalization.** The traditional approach to file design focuses entirely on the needs of a specific application (i.e., a group of related processing requirements). Data required by more than one application is often duplicated rather than shared, and storage and access decisions are made to optimize the files for the primary user.

In a data base environment, however, the emphasis on managing data as a corporate resource changes the data base into a repository of shared information. Thus, customized representations or implementations are inappropriate. Evaluating cost and performance in such an environment is complex, since the overall objective is a kind of global optimum that may be suboptimal for any given application or primary user.

**Extent of Required Analysis.** For most data bases, some degree of analysis is worthwhile, considering the often severe and continuing penalties resulting from inefficient implementation. The effort involved in such analysis, however, must be weighed against its benefit. When selecting a data compression method for a textural data base, for example, the designer should determine whether the cost of content analysis is justified or whether similar information is available in published works on character frequency in English text.

**Application and Configuration Requirements.** When matching the structural and utilization requirements of the data base with the capabilities of the DBMS as well as with available access methods and data storage devices, the data base designer should attempt to make an economic trade-off between the power of the configuration and the requirements of the applications. The configuration should meet the requirements without providing significant unused capacity.

**Planning for the Future.** The data base designer should try to select a design that will remain tenable for a number of years. To do so, the designer must consider the life expectancy of the data base as well as current trends in DBMS software and data storage devices. For example, the storage and access potential of new devices (e.g., mass storage devices, bubble memories) and new data structuring ideas (e.g., relational and set-theoretic data models) should not be overlooked.

**Planned versus Ad Hoc Processing.** The data base designer must know the required proportion of planned to ad hoc processing. Design decisions favoring planned processing put less emphasis on nonprocedural interaction with the data base than do those supporting spontaneous processing. Similarly, the storage overhead (e.g., indexes, pointers) necessary to facilitate ad hoc processing is unnecessarily burdensome when applications are known and repeated.

## OPERATIONAL TRADE-OFFS

There are operational trade-offs during both logical and physical design. During logical design, operational trade-offs relate primarily to the strategies and tools selected for developing the data base schema. During physical design, the trade-offs concern alternatives for data base implementation. Certain operational trade-offs relate to the interaction between logical and physical design.

### Trade-offs in Logical Design

The logical design phase begins with an investigation of user requirements and ends with a logical description (schema) of a data base that can support those requirements. This description, termed logical because it does not contain details about how the data is to be represented, is used during the subsequent physical design phase.

Logical design can be divided into four activities [1]:
* Requirements analysis
* Data modeling
* View integration
* Schema development
The breakdown is shown in Figure 4-1.

Requirements analysis is the process of determining and documenting user needs. These needs are then expressed as an abstract, formal data model that represents the user's environment as realistically as possible. Since the data base must support a number of users, each with different views of the data, several views must be integrated into one global data model. The global data model is then transformed into a DBMS-dependent schema representation.

Logical design decisions have an immediate effect on how data is collected and assembled to meet user needs. When making these decisions, the logical designer faces several trade-offs.

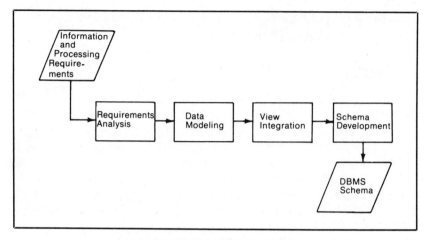

**Figure 4-1. The Logical Design Phase**

**Application versus Global Modeling.** Two activities in logical design—data modeling and view integration—reflect the designer's attempt to model each user's view, or application, separately and then to merge these views into a global model capable of supporting all users. Although this approach makes the collection of user requirements and model development easier, there is no guarantee that the view models can be successfully integrated. Since the development of the full data base can occur over time (i.e., when applications are added in succession), incompatibility of application models can necessitate costly data base redesign.

To avoid this problem, the designer can initially develop a global model and define application models as subsets of the global model. In order to develop a global model, however, the requirements analysis must also be global in scope. This increases the complexity of the design task as well as the time and resources required to accomplish the task. In addition, such an approach delays the expected benefit of the data base implementation because no applications can be put into production until the full data base is specified.

Most designers believe a compromise in which a high-level global model is developed [5] and used as a guide during the specification of application models is the solution. Such an approach can reduce the risk of incompatibility without adding inordinately to the complexity and cost of the design process.

**Choosing a Data Modeling Technique.** There are many data modeling techniques [6], all of which contain constructs and notations for representing data entities and relationships. In choosing a modeling technique, the designer must weigh capabilities in requirements specification and user communication against the ease of mapping models developed with the technique into appropriate DBMS schemas. Generally, the more user oriented the technique (i.e., the easier it is to represent and interpret its models), the less rigorous and complete it is. Thus, models of this type must be augmented and revised before they are mapped to DBMS schemas.

**Process- versus Information-Oriented Design.** The traditional approach to data file design emphasizes processing requirements rather than data. Only those data elements required by the processing are included and are grouped to optimize efficient execution of the processes required. Although exclusive use of this approach is inappropriate in a data base environment, the degree to which processing requirements should influence data base design is still in question.

This trade-off represents a balance between completeness and adequacy. A complete data base must contain all information relevant to the organization (i.e., a faithful and complete model). A complete data base is perfectly flexible (i.e., able to support all existing and future processing needs) at the cost of excess data collection and maintenance. A data base designed with a process orientation, however, contains only that data necessary to make it adequate for support of processing requirements. Although a customized data base is less costly initially, it requires redefinition when inadequate for new processing requirements.

**DBMS-Dependent versus DBMS-Independent Design.** When to introduce the DBMS into the data base design process is an important concern of the data base designer. Many believe that to achieve short-range efficiency, the logical constructs of the DBMS should be used as early as the requirements specification and data modeling stages. In this way, all information needed for the DBMS data base schema would be collected and extraneous information would not. A data model expressed in DBMS constructs cannot easily be mapped into the constructs of another DBMS, however; additional analysis and design work are necessary if the software environment changes. In addition, each DBMS imposes its own logical view of how data should be grouped and structured. The designer who follows this view early in the logical design phase can miss opportunities for representing data requirements that may, in the long run, surpass those offered by the DBMS.

## Trade-offs in Physical Design

The physical design phase begins with a logical schema that represents user requirements and provides information on the processing requirements. A plan for the physical implementation of the data base that will achieve the best performance at the least cost results. Physical design includes four activities:
- Determining and documenting data representation
- Selecting and documenting access modes
- Allocating data to devices
- Loading and reorganizing the data base

These physical design activities are represented in Figure 4-2.

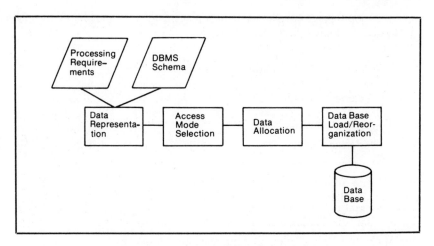

**Figure 4-2. The Physical Design Phase**

Each data element and group in the schema is first assigned a data type and size and is then documented using the data definition language (DDL) of the DBMS. Next, the access methods by which the elements and records will be stored and retrieved are chosen. Each element, record, or file is then assigned to a data storage device, and these assignments are recorded in the DBMS internal schema [5], using Device Media Control Language (DMCL). Finally, the physical designer loads the actual data into the data base and prepares to revise the decisions concerning physical aspects of the data base as changes in data or processing requirements dictate.

During physical design, data storage and processing costs must be weighed against data base performance. Unfortunately, improvements in cost usually deter performance; improvements in performance generally increase cost.

**Effect of Data Allocation.** Access to data on secondary storage devices is efficient when data that is used together is stored in close physical proximity. Clustering data in this way improves the chances that a physical block of data transferred to main memory will have more than one required data record. When multiple blocks must be retrieved, I/O time can be minimized if access is restricted to tracks within one disk cylinder or those on adjacent cylinders.

The trade-off here is that while data base environment processing programs share data, the optimal data allocation for each is likely to differ. The physical designer must plan data allocation in response to application priorities, based on a minimum standard for acceptable performance for each application.

**Choosing an Access Method.** Many DBMSs offer the designer a choice of access methods for each physical file in the data base. When selecting an access method, the designer must determine whether to trade storage efficiency and access method simplicity for flexibility and speed of data access. Methods with minimal storage and processing overhead (e.g., a sequential-access method) place constraints on data placement (e.g., the requirement for a physical or logical sequence of records) and processing (e.g., no direct record retrieval or in-place updating). Methods that allow flexible and direct retrieval (e.g., indexed or inverted list methods) require additional storage (e.g., for pointers, indexes, directories) and more complex processing operations (e.g., for overflow handling or record addition and deletion).

**Redundancy versus Efficiency.** Although minimal redundancy is an objective of the data base approach, with current hardware and software, controlled redundancy may be necessary and desirable for efficient processing. A data element such as PROD-NAME, shown in Figure 4-3, should ideally be stored once within a data base, probably with the other attributes of the product it describes. An order referring to this product might contain the product identifier, but the product name would not be stored redundantly. Duplicating the PROD-NAME data element as an attribute of the order, however, may save enough I/O accesses to more than offset the cost of the additional bytes of storage. The physical designer must think about such trade-offs explicitly and ensure that proper controls are in place to guarantee consistency among duplicate instances of the same data element. In the preceding example, an update to the product data involving PROD-NAME must trigger a similar update of related orders.

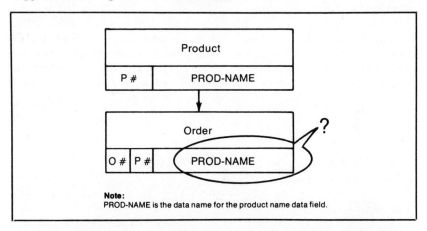

**Figure 4-3. Redundancy versus Efficiency: Should Product Name Be Stored Twice?**

**Data Compression.** Compressing, or compacting, data before it is stored can save valuable storage space. This is especially important in conjunction with access methods (e.g., inverted lists) that add substantial overhead information to the data base. This saving in storage must be weighed against increased processing time for encoding or decoding data elements when adding them to or deleting them from the data base. The balance can be tipped in favor of data compression by selective compression. With selective compression, only certain portions of the data (e.g., non-key fields) are compressed;

thus, many searches can be performed without decoding until the final set of records is selected.

## Interaction between Logical and Physical Design

Although logical and physical design are two distinct phases of the data base design process, they affect each other. The designer must be aware of this and must know how the interaction can affect data base structure and implementation.

**DBMS Constraints on Physical Design.** Ideally, the constructs used to represent the logical schema for a data base are independent of implementation details. In most commercial DBMSs, however, this ideal is not achieved. The constructs used to represent groups of related data items (e.g., records or segments) actually represent physically stored records. In addition, the relationships described define actual access paths, and, in some cases, data allocation is specified in the data base schema (e.g., the CODASYL Data Base Task Group—DBTG) area or realm concept. When this type of overlap occurs, the physical designer has less flexibility in selecting implementation methods. Furthermore, a change in implementation has far-reaching ramifications because the logical schema and programs based on that schema may be affected.

**Impact of Processing Optimization on Logical Design.** Concern for the performance of data base applications can result in constraints on the logical design. The designer may choose to use only those DBMS constructs or relationships that are known to provide fast access. For example, an IMS designer may express most data base views as independent (physical) data bases, choosing not to use the IMS facility that allows a logical view to span two or more physical data bases. Another example is the DBTG designer who chooses to avoid the DBTG set type and, instead, represents the relationship between two types of records using embedded (and redundant) data values. Unfortunately, allowing physical considerations to constrain the logical design obviates the benefits of data independence and prevents the logical designer and application programmers from taking full advantage of the power of the DBMS.

The effects of logical design on physical design and vice versa appear to result from shortcomings in currently available DBMSs and storage devices. Advances in either area should promote true data independence, thus eliminating these trade-offs.

## CONCLUSION

The two classes of trade-offs discussed in this chapter generally relate to the phases of the data base design process (see Figure 4-4). General trade-offs are applicable throughout the design process; operational trade-offs are encountered in the more analytical steps that follow the data base design phases.

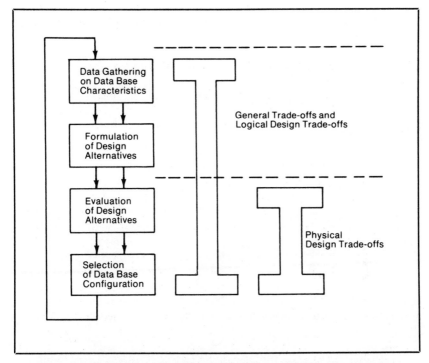

**Figure 4-4. The Relationship of General and Operational Trade-offs to the
Data Base Design Process**

During the formulation of alternative designs, the general trade-offs can be
used by the data base designer in three ways:

- To set practical limits on the resources (i.e., personnel, time, funds)
  expended on the design process. This function is served primarily by
  the trade-off involving the extent of analysis performed.
- To provide guidance whenever choices must be made. For example,
  the generality of a particular data modeling technique may result in its
  recommendation, or a device may be rejected for lack of desired capabilities.
- To aid in developing an acceptance standard (or a set of criteria) that
  can be used to evaluate operational trade-offs. For example, to be
  acceptable, a design may be required to meet retrieval needs for a
  period of five years.

Results of the operational trade-offs in logical design provide the data base
designer with a logical design approach and tool(s) for specifying data requirements. The approach selected determines the scope of the logical design
process and the types and extent of data collected during this phase. The data
model selected and its relationship to the DBMS further define the type of
requirements data to be collected and also govern whether or not a schema
mapping step is necessary as part of logical design.

Ideally, the data base designer should be able to evaluate the operational trade-offs among alternative physical configurations in an iterative fashion. The designer should be able to change design parameters and easily reevaluate each alternative. He or she should also be able to stratify the evaluation of a given data base (i.e., apply different constraints and design alternatives to different portions of the data base). It should be possible, for example, to evaluate the effect of using a mix of devices (i.e., a storage hierarchy). The best way to accomplish a systematic evaluation of this type is to simulate or model the data base in question [7].

In any case, the evaluation of the operational trade-offs for each design alternative should result in the identification of one or more designs that meet the acceptance standard. If only one configuration is acceptable, selection is complete. If more than one meets the standard, a final decision is required. The designer may again rely on the priorities established by the general trade-offs to aid in the final selection. For example, if two equally acceptable designs differ in ad hoc inquiry support, the planned versus ad hoc processing trade-off could be the determining factor.

Once selected and implemented, a data base design should be monitored over its lifetime to ensure that it continues to meet the criteria that resulted in its selection. Both classes of trade-offs should continue to guide the data base designer and should serve as indicators of the need for redesign.

References

1. Yao, S.B., Navathe, S.B., and Weldon, J.L. "An Integrated Approach to Logical Data Base Design." *Proceedings of the NYU Symposium on Data Base Design*. New York, 1978.
2. Martin, J. *Computer Data Base Organization*. Englewood Cliffs NJ: Prentice-Hall Inc, 1975.
3. Date, C.J. *An Introduction to Database Systems*. Reading MA: Addison-Wesley, 1977.
4. Weldon, J.L. *Data Base Administration*. New York: Plenum Publishing Co, 1981.
5. *ANSI/X3/SPARC Study Group on Data Base Management Systems*. Seattle WA: Interim Report 75-02-08. ACM FDT Vol. 7, No. 2 (1975).
6. Wiederhold, G. *Database Design*. New York: McGraw-Hill, 1977.
7. Weldon, J.L. *Data Storage Decisions for Large Data Bases*. Springfield VA: NTIS Publication No. AS/A-023874. U.S. Department of Commerce, February 1976.

# 5 Systems Development in a Data Base Environment
by Bernard K. Plagman

## INTRODUCTION

The seventies witnessed the maturation of data base technology. Data base management systems (DBMSs), which in earlier years were prone to software errors, became relatively bug free and comparatively stable. Tools to support the development and operation of information systems built on the principle of data shared among different applications became available. Instead of being used as a sophisticated access method, DBMSs and other data base technologies began to be employed as integral and important parts of a data base environment.

This chapter defines the term "data base environment" and explores the impact of the data base phenomenon on systems development. Because the systems development process is fundamentally affected by the principle of data sharing, this chapter discusses the areas of management and control of that process that merit close attention. In particular, the use of the Data Dictionary/Directory System (DD/DS) is stressed because it has considerable potential as a tool for developing better management practices and more effective project control.

It should be noted that this chapter discusses the impact of a technical issue—data base technology—on a management process—systems development. The purpose is not to dwell on the technical aspects but to focus on areas that affect management of the systems development process. Thus, this chapter focuses on the role of systems development, the fundamentals of the data base environment, the impact of that environment on the systems development process, and the control concerns of the DP manager.

## ROLE OF SYSTEMS DEVELOPMENT

Systems development is responsible for software development projects that entail designing, implementing, and maintaining information systems in response to users' business needs. Typically, this function reports to the DP manager, and many application development projects may be under its control. For the purpose of this discussion, it is assumed that systems development is responsible for two or more application development projects.

The basic role and management objectives of systems development are constant, regardless of the technologies used in the implementation of information systems. Systems development's role is to apply and effectively manage resources to achieve management goals. The objective is to deliver to the end user information systems that provide accurate, consistent, complete, and timely information, consistent with the end user's business needs. This must be accomplished within budgeted limits for time, money, and personnel.

While role and management objectives are unaffected by the use of specific technologies, the way the systems manager performs duties and functions is most definitely affected. In a data base environment, certain aspects of the development process must be emphasized; coordinating activity becomes more important, as does the use of standard practices. In addition, technical expertise applied at key points in the development process is indispensable in a data base environment.

In order to more fully explain the impact of the data base environment on systems development, it is helpful to describe that environment.

## DATA BASE ENVIRONMENT

A data base environment can be defined by the information systems it supports and the hardware/software and administrative components of which it consists.

Information systems in a data base environment share data by means of a data base to increase accuracy and consistency of representation. In a bank system employing dedicated files, for example, both redundancy and inconsistency of data may occur (see Figure 5-1). The shared use of data in a data base, however, helps alleviate these problems (see Figure 5-2). This sharing of data to build integrated information systems is a characteristic that distinguishes a data base environment from conventionally designed systems.

There are five basic components of a data base environment:
- Data base—a collection of data logically organized to meet the information requirements of a universe of users
- Data base management system—a hardware/software system that manages data by providing organization, access, and control functions
- Data Dictionary/Directory System—a repository of information about data and the data base environment
- User system interfaces—components of the data base environment that request, manipulate, and transform data into information for end users
- Data base administration—A human function involved in the coordination and control of data-related activities

The first four items are hardware/software components; the fifth is administrative. Figure 5-3 shows the functional architecture of this environment and illustrates the interaction between components.

It is important to recognize that the components of the data base environment support multiple logical views of a single physical representation of

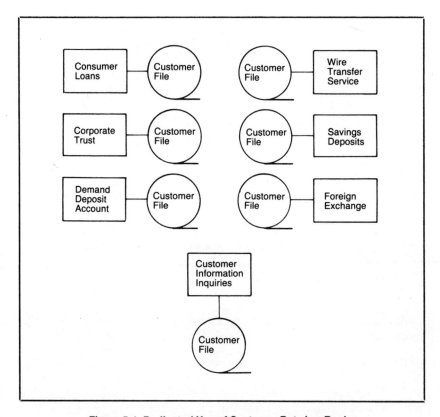

Figure 5-1. Dedicated Use of Customer Data in a Bank

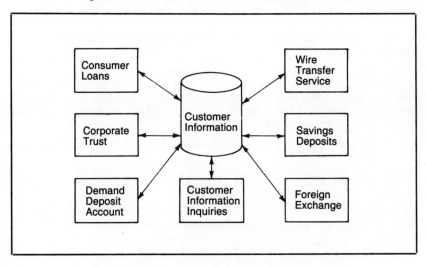

Figure 5-2. Sample Data Base of Information for a Bank

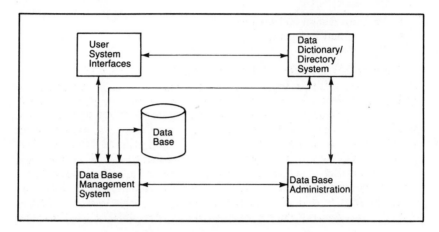

**Figure 5-3. Functions Performed in a Data Base Environment**

data. This capability, which is necessary to support data sharing among diverse applications, is accomplished at the technical level through data independence techniques.

At the application program level, each program is provided with a data description that represents the program's logical view of data. The DBMS is given a data description corresponding to the global logical view that satisfies all logical views. In addition, the DBMS is furnished with the description of the physical representation in terms of storage structures and access methods necessary to support the global logical view. Thus, there is a set of separate but consistent definitions that describes the multiple logical views as well as the single physical representation used in data sharing among application systems.

## IMPACT OF A DATA BASE ENVIRONMENT ON SYSTEMS DEVELOPMENT

The impact of a data base environment on systems development depends upon the level of data sharing. The higher the level of sharing, the greater the impact on the systems development life cycle (SDLC); the lower the level of sharing, the less the impact.

### Systems Development Life Cycle

The systems development life cycle aids in managing and controlling development activities. Projects are hierarchically structured into units of work called phases, activities, tasks, and sometimes even smaller units of work. A data base environment affects the SDLC at the phase level.

The SDLC consists of five phases:
- Requirements analysis and feasibility
- Systems design

- Program design and coding
- Testing and acceptance
- Operations and maintenance

These phases are affected by a data base environment because of the contrast between file design and data base design. File design is typically an application-project-oriented task under the direct auspices of a project leader; it yields files primarily dedicated to specified purposes. The data base design process, on the other hand, results in a data base that can be shared among many applications with diverse logical views. This requirement for data sharing necessitates two separate but interdependent design processes that must proceed in parallel—systems design and data base design. The systems development process must therefore interact with the data base design process. This interaction must be defined in terms of a data base development life cycle, just as the systems design is defined in terms of a systems development life cycle.

The data base development life cycle (also referred to as a data base design methodology) consists of four major phases:

- Global conceptual data base design—identifies entities and the data clusters that describe these entities. It also includes specifying relationships among the data clusters defined. The result is a global conceptual data structure diagram and supporting documentation.
- Detailed conceptual data base design—follows the global phase of design and uses its deliverables. This phase entails specifying record types, including design and assignment of data elements. The result of this phase is a detailed conceptual data structure diagram and supporting documentation.
- Logical data base design—is based on logical view requirements developed in application projects, uses the detailed conceptual design, and adds storage structures and access methods that can satisfy all logical views. The result is a global logical data base, which may include a data structure diagram and data description language (DDL) code as well as supporting documentation.
- Physical data base design—allocates storage for the data base and determines such physical aspects as buffer and block sizes and physical placement options. The result of this phase is a fully described data base design coded and ready for data base loading procedures.

Figure 5-4 illustrates the manner in which the phases of the SDLC must interact with the phases of the data base development life cycle. Most important from the systems development viewpoint is the responsibility to deliver the definition of logical views and to critically review the deliverables provided by the data base design process. The interaction of the phases of the SDLC with those of the data base development life cycle is discussed in the following paragraphs.

**Requirements Analysis and Feasibility.** During this initial SDLC phase, efforts focus on user-oriented and conceptual aspects of the design; it is important to coordinate these activities with the development of the global

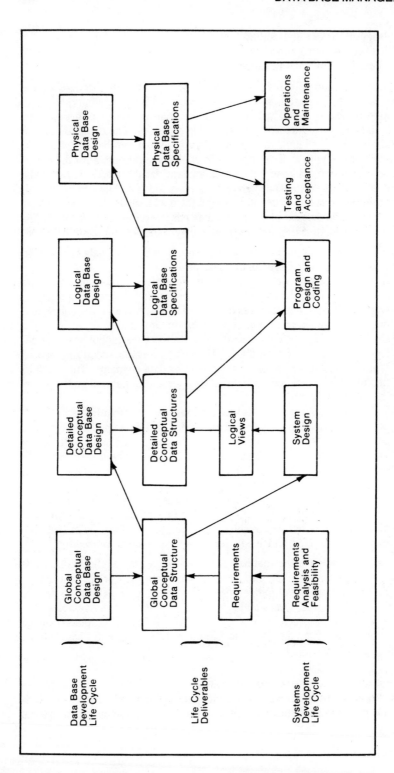

**Figure 5-4. Interaction between Data Base Development Life Cycle and Systems Development Life Cycle**

conceptual data structure. This data structure should be produced in an independent planning effort that precedes the initiation of an SDLC for the application project. An application project thus deals with a subset of the global conceptual data structure and refines the applicable sections of that structure in accordance with user requirements by providing additional conceptual insight. In this regard, systems development is responsible for ensuring that each application is appropriately placed into the context of the overall global conceptual data structure.

One question concerning the feasibility of an application project is whether it can use the data base(s) defined in the global conceptual data structure and whether supporting data base technology (e.g., a DBMS) must be employed. These issues should be formally addressed in the requirements and feasibility report. In addition, this report should identify and describe user requirements that are related to the access, storage, and maintenance of information in the data base(s).

**Systems Design.** The second phase of the SDLC is concerned with detailed analysis leading to a systems solution. The systems design effort is a refinement of the previous phase, which established only feasibility for the conceptual level.

The systems development manager must be sure that each application project specifies its data requirements in conjunction with the detailed specification stage of systems design (i.e., the logical views of each application must be carefully detailed). This is accomplished by enumerating the transactions needed to support the business functions in question. From these transactions, the analysis identifies the data elements and data relationships necessary to support the application. The need for retrieving, updating, and modifying data is established and corresponding volume-frequency information compiled. This data should then be analyzed and prepared as a formal deliverable representing the logical views of the application.

**Program Design and Coding.** This SDLC phase involves the transformation of the systems design into operable code. The tasks in this phase usually require knowledge of the data structures and access methods used in the data base design. Thus, information from the data base design process must be made available to the systems development project team. This information is delivered in the form of the logical data base design.

In the course of designing and coding application programs, systems development personnel should employ procedures and techniques to promote data independence and the overall integrity of the data base. Special care should be applied when writing programs that update, modify, and/or delete data from the data base. In addition, special attention should be given to edit and validation controls, DBMS return-code processing, and other error processing procedures.

**Testing and Acceptance.** During this phase, the system undergoes various levels of testing to ensure design completeness and accuracy. If data is shared across application lines, however, an additional level of testing—data base integration testing—must be performed, during which the newly coded application system is processed against a test data base, along with the other application programs that are in production mode. This is done in order to verify that the newly coded programs will not have an adverse impact on existing programs.

**Operations and Maintenance.** The final phase of the SDLC is an ongoing phase—the production mode of operations and the method for correcting bugs and enhancing the application systems.

Maintenance is critical in a data base environment. Changes to data elements can affect several application programs, thus crossing application project boundaries. Of course, this situation can be mitigated if a reasonable degree of data independence has been ensured in previous phases of the SDLC. A high degree of data independence permits changes in data elements while circumventing actual coding changes. In many instances, recompilation of application programs can be avoided. A reasonable degree of program data independence can also significantly reduce the relative percentage of manpower and other resources expended on maintenance versus new development.

The interaction and coordination of the systems and data base life cycles is controlled by the deliverables that serve as interfaces between the two life cycles. As illustrated in Figure 5-4, the deliverables of each life cycle play an important role in all subsequent phases.

## CONTROL CONCERNS OF SYSTEMS DEVELOPMENT

Controls are implemented in information systems in order to ensure the accuracy, completeness, and timeliness of information provided to end users. The system of internal control also helps ensure authorized access and adequate audit trails. Automated controls must be considered part of the system of internal control. Development projects must also be controlled to ensure their completion on time and within budget.

### Development Project Control

A data base design project must have its own centralized administration. The systems development manager, therefore, must ensure that controls for the systems development project are not neglected. In the traditional environment, project leaders had total control over the development effort, inclusive of file design; in the data base environment, however, the project leader must rely on data base designers who will probably work in a separate organizational unit (e.g., Data Base Administration [DBA]). In a data base environment, therefore, "finger pointing" may arise between members of the project team and those of the data base design team. Although the purpose of the DBA function is to coordinate and control, quality control and timely completion of project activities remain a systems management responsibility.

## Design and Implementation of Controls in Systems

Information systems supported by a data base environment raise new control concerns and also present opportunities to mitigate them.

One of the greatest problems in a data base environment is the migration of system controls from the individual application to the generalized systems environment. Access controls to prevent unauthorized reading and writing to files may be an application program function in a traditional environment. In a data base environment, however, these controls are implemented in the context of the data base management system as part of the security mechanism available on a general basis. This is true for other types of controls as well, including edit and validation, restart/recovery, and contention controls.

The migration of controls affects systems development in a number of important ways. It particularly affects placement and awareness of controls.

**Placement of Controls.** The placement of controls in the design is usually heavily influenced by the systems designer. In addition, placement has a direct impact on the controls' effectiveness as well as on any cost benefit analysis that might be performed to evaluate them.

The opportunity for efficient and effective placement of controls is greatly enhanced in a data base environment. Among the numerous possibilities are:
- Schema/subschema controls
- Privacy locks and keys
- Before/after image logging
- Data base procedures

**Awareness of Control Requirements.** Even in a non-data-base environment, the systems manager must be mindful of the need for controls in automated information systems. In a data base environment, however, the control concerns are heightened because of the introduction of data sharing and the implementation of data independence. This has brought about greater concern in the areas of authorized access, coordination of activity, and concentration of risk.

It is the systems manager's responsibility to ensure that designers are aware of the need for controls. Furthermore, the opportunities for using new tools and techniques should be underscored in order to guarantee that all available alternatives are evaluated.

The best way to promote an awareness of these control issues among designers is through training sessions. The efficacy of such training is enhanced by the participation of a member of the EDP auditing staff.

## Personnel Considerations

A lack of necessary technical support skills is possibly the most common cause of delays and even failure of projects involving data base management.

Moreover, these technical skills are most important during the initial phases of design, a time when staff is just "getting their feet wet."

The following skills are necessary in the systems staff to support the design and implementation of data-base-supported information systems:
- Specification of logical views of data
- Design of data structures
- Knowledge of DBMS-specific access methods
- Data manipulation coding techniques
- Knowledge of DBMS-specific performance analysis

The systems manager should plan and initiate training sessions to ensure that the design staff has the required skills to operate effectively. Many organizations use outside consultants to provide the required skills. The systems manager should choose consultants who employ proven data base design methodologies.

### Using the DD/DS As a Tool for Management and Control

The following briefly summarizes some of the ways a DD/DS can assist in managing and controlling the data base environment.

**Documentation.** The DD/DS can assist in maintaining up-to-date and reliable descriptions of the programs and modules that share portions of the data base. Documentation can be produced as a by-product of the development process instead of as a burdensome addition.

**Controlling Change.** The DD/DS can help ensure accurate and authorized changes to the systems environment. By using the STATUS attribute provided in most DD/DSs, systems managers can effectively track and control changes to programs and data descriptions within their purview.

**SDLC Support.** The management objective of requiring deliverables for each phase of the SDLC can be greatly facilitated by the DD/DS. The DD/DS can collect the data necessary for each deliverable and then produce the information necessary to create each of these deliverables (see Figure 5-5). The DD/DS can be employed to generate data structure diagrams at various phases of the SDLC, for example.

### CONCLUSION

The introduction of data sharing and the implementation of data independence affects systems development by:
- Changing the SDLC
- Increasing control concerns
- Affecting project management
- Requiring highly skilled personnel

| Systems Development Life Cycles | | |
|---|---|---|
| Systems Development | Data Base Development | DD/DS |
| Needs Identification Feasibility Functional Specification | Needs Identification Global Conceptual Design | Documentation and Analytic Support |
| System Specification Programming Specification | Detailed Conceptual Design | Documentation and Analytic Support Change Control |
| Programming Unit and Integration Testing | Logical Design Physical Design | Metadata Generation Change Control Metadata Generation Change Control |
| Conversion Operation | Operation Maintenance | Metadata Generation Change Control |

Figure 5-5. DD/DS Interface of Systems Development Life Cycles

A program should be undertaken to prepare the systems environment for the introduction of data base technology. This program can include:

- Intensive training in the concepts, methods, and procedures of designing data base-supported information systems
- Employment of outside consultation and expertise when appropriate
- Consideration of the DD/DS as an aid in managing and controlling the environment

Finally, data base technology should be adopted on a phased implementation basis.

# ⑥ Restart and Recovery in DBMSs

by J. Chris Wood

## INTRODUCTION

As organizations continue to investigate the benefits of integrating data bases, protecting data files has become more important. Many benefits of using DP techniques can best be realized when all, or a significant portion, of the organization's data resources are integrated under the control of a DBMS. Many critical applications thus depend on the DBMS to provide a constantly available and accurate source of data. To meet this need, a DBMS must contain basic functions that can detect and recover from any type of failure in as short a time as possible and still be able to handle the processing load dependent on the data. Without such functions, a DBMS will quickly gain a reputation of unreliability or excessive downtime. Users will then ask to have their data isolated for better reliability, undermining the concept of sharing data. Thus, the effectiveness of restart and recovery mechanisms is an important consideration in creating a successful data base environment.

This chapter discusses in detail the design considerations and trade-offs that must be considered when developing restart/recovery procedures. Because recovery is an important criterion in the selection of a DBMS, the information in this chapter can also be used during the evaluation phase of that process.

## RECOVERY CONCEPTS

The basic goal of recovery is to provide a framework within which a damaged data base can be restored to its former contents. This concept can involve a series of manual and/or automated procedures. The basic trade-off is between throughput efficiency and recovery efficiency.

### Recovery Tools

Four basic tools are used in the recovery of a data base:
- Transaction log/journal
- Before and after images
- Save/restore (dumps)

- Checkpoints

A DBMS must incorporate all four tools to have an adequate recovery mechanism.

**Transaction Log/Journal.** For recovery purposes, this log contains a copy of each update transaction against the data base. It may also contain read-only transactions, statistics, beginning- and end-of-transaction entries, checkpoint indicators, and before and after images.

**Before and After Images.** A before image is a copy of a portion of the data base before it is updated. An after image is a copy of a portion of the data base after it is modified. Both types of image are stored on either the transaction log or a separate log file. A data base update using these images must be performed in the following sequences:

1. Write before image to log
2. Write after image to log
3. Write after image to data base (perform update)
4. Mark log to reflect successful completion of update (optional)

This procedure guarantees that the log always reflects the data base and that all updates to the data base can be recreated or removed, depending on the type of recovery.

Not every update to the data base will generate four I/O operations. In most DBMSs, several before images might be written for a given record before the after images are written. This idea is explained further in the discussion of granularity later in this chapter. In addition, most DBMSs buffer the before and after images to reduce the number of physical I/O operations. The previous sequence must still be maintained, however; for example, no after image may be written to the data base until the buffer containing a copy of that after image has been successfully written to a log file, regardless of the amount of data currently in the buffer.

**Save/Restore.** Saving the data base entails copying it at some time; restoring a data base involves recreating it from a saved copy. Some DBMSs allow partial saves and restorations of sections of a data base. This procedure should be used carefully (if at all) and only under specific conditions with explicit controls; otherwise, unsynchronized data can compromise the integrity and reliability of the data base. Procedures to ensure integrity and reliability in case of partial restorations are especially critical in systems that use internal physical pointers between records. For example, it is possible to save a section of a data base that points to a record, which is deleted before the section containing that record is saved. When the two sections are restored, any program using that relationship will abort.

**Checkpoint.** A checkpoint in a data base environment occurs when no updates are in progress; thus, it is certain that the data base is intact. A checkpoint is typically achieved by:

- Halting all incoming transactions or queuing them
- Writing all before and after images still in the log buffer to the log
- Writing all modified pages from the data base buffers
- Marking the log

Checkpoints can also be established at the individual transaction, or program, level. In this technique, the DBMS controls the use of each record in the data base through some internal flagging algorithm. The DBMS guarantees that only one transaction can update a record at a given instant by locking that record. This lock can be removed only when the transaction owning the lock terminates normally or issues a command to release all of its locked records. Because a locked record cannot be accessed by another transaction, transactions needing a locked record are queued until that record is unlocked. This technique guarantees that each transaction has a private subset of the data base (identified by its locks) and can therefore be considered a unit for checkpoint purposes. For the duration of a given transaction, no other transaction could have possibly changed any data updated by this transaction; thus, any roll-forward or rollback operations would not affect other transactions. This form of checkpointing requires start-of-transaction, end-of-transaction, and checkpoint records to be written to the same log file as the before and after images.

## TYPES OF FAILURE

Five types of failure can occur in a data base environment; each requires different combinations of mechanisms for recovery:

- Catastrophic—portion of data base unreadable
- Intermittent—data base stopped, status of last transactions unknown
- Transaction failure
- Valid but incorrect update—data base erosion
- Structural damage—failure of pointer mechanisms

**Catastrophic Failure.** With this type of failure, all or part of the data base is unreadable, typically as a result of I/O device errors. Because the data base is unreadable, recovery must begin with a purge of the bad data and restoration of a previous copy of the data base. Recovery must roll this file forward until it duplicates the data in the original, undamaged data base.

The first step in this process is to destroy the damaged data base. Next, an old copy of the saved data base is restored to the disk. The more often a save is performed, the more recent is this copy of the data base and the speedier the recovery.

The next step involves rolling the data base forward in time. After images are written to the new file in ascending time sequence (i.e., oldest to newest), applying all modifications to the data base in the exact sequence in which they occurred. The transactions that generated the changes are unknown, however. Since some transactions may not have been completed before the damage was detected, not every after image on the log file can be applied. Some data, or pointers, could have been modified in the data buffers but never written to the file, for example. Thus, this method can only recover up to the most recent checkpoint. Checkpoint recovery, which is neither simple nor straightforward, is detailed in the next section.

**Intermittent Failure.** This occurs when activity to the data base is suddenly interrupted without a chance to perform a checkpoint or allow currently executing transactions to finish. Although the entire data base is readable when the system is reactivated, it is still damaged; it cannot be known whether modifications still in the buffer or in a given program were made to the data in the data base.

Because a readable but inaccurate copy of the data base exists, there is no need to purge it. Instead, recovery from this type of failure consists of taking the damaged data base and rolling it backward to the most recent checkpoint. The checkpoint could have occurred only when no transactions were in progress and the buffers were flushed or written to the file.

Rolling back the file to the previous checkpoint involves writing before images to the data base in reverse time sequence; thus, all modifications since the last checkpoint are backed out. Either the log file is read backward or the last checkpoint is found; then all before images up to the failure are copied, sorted in reverse time sequence, and written directly to the file. An alternative approach is to apply only the before images of incomplete transactions.

Many systems now have a recovery feature that enables the system to automatically roll back to the previous checkpoint when it restarts after intermittent failure. This is advantageous because it removes a human function from the process. Systems that automatically roll forward should be carefully examined to determine how they reexecute the transaction that caused the failure (e.g., potential infinite loop recoveries must be avoided).

**Transaction Failure.** This occurs when a transaction fails after updating one or more records in the data base. Recovery is similar to that for intermittent failure, except that only before images for the records modified by the failed transaction are applied to the data. In most cases, other transactions currently executing are allowed to continue—even during recovery for the failed transaction. At the end of the rollback, all locks held by the failed transaction are released. This erases all impact on the data base generated by the failed transaction so that the transaction appears to have never existed.

**Valid but Incorrect Update.** This is typically detected by a user who notes some discrepancy in a report after an update. No edit/validation procedure can guarantee detection of all errors (e.g., transposing numbers or entering too many zeros at the end of a numeric field). Recovery from this condition could be performed ideally by processing the data base to the nearest checkpoint and then rerunning all transactions since that time. After images could not be used because they contain the incorrect update.

To limit the scope of recovery, all areas of the data base affected by the modification must be carefully tracked, as should all modifications made by transactions reading this changed data. The longer the time period involved, the less feasible this requirement becomes. Furthermore, the expense of logging all transactions read to the data base creates a large overhead that may be difficult to justify.

Although the most common answer to the problem is to enter a counter transaction to correct the data, this solution does not encompass cascaded transactions (i.e., transactions that read the incorrect base and used it to update data elsewhere). Because tracking cascaded transactions is so complex, no effective general solution has been found; in fact, very little effort has been expended searching for one. Proper use of a data dictionary or directory system, however, can simplify tracking the cascade effect and identifying affected users.

**Structural Damage.** This problem is caused by a failure of the pointer mechanisms within a data base. Specifically, a pointer stored in a record incorrectly points to either unrelated or nonexistent data. This is usually not detected when it occurs but when a transaction attempting to follow this pointer aborts.

Occasionally this condition can be corrected by some form of direct modification utility that can be applied to the data base without being controlled by the DBMS. This is a dangerous utility that must be carefully used and controlled.

If direct fixes cannot be applied, the data base must be recovered to the most recent checkpoint before the damage occurred. The same techniques used for the other types of failures can be employed.

The remainder of this chapter concentrates primarily on the catastrophic and intermittent failures and the basic tools to recover from them. Recovery from incorrect data and/or pointers uses these same basic tools after the initial repair; however, the difficulty of tracking cascaded transactions and the possibility that the error has existed for a long time before detection make generalized recovery from these situations extremely difficult, if not impossible.

## RECOVERY DESIGN CONSIDERATIONS

Many factors should be considered when evaluating or designing a data base recovery mechanism. The primary trade-off is usually between speed of recovery and efficiency of throughput. Typically, techniques allowing the fastest recovery tend to impose the most overhead on the system during normal processing. The following section discusses the most important design considerations for recovery software.

### Checkpoints/Dumps

Frequency is an important consideration in making backup copies of the data base. If the interval between save commands is $n$ minutes, a catastrophic failure requires recovery time proportional to that needed to execute an average of $n/2$ minutes of processing. Since writing after images is much more efficient than performing all transactions for the period, the actual time of recovery is less than $n/2$ minutes. It is therefore important to minimize the time between dumps. While a save command is running, however, no updates can be allowed to the data base. Depending on the size of the data base, this restriction could significantly delay update processing. The ability to save or restore several sections of the data base simultaneously could lessen the impact (at the expense of complicating the procedure).

The frequency of checkpoints involves the same trade-off as dump frequency; recovery is faster the more frequently a checkpoint is taken, but a heavier burden is placed on throughput. For a given purpose, the longer the time between checkpoints, the more before and after images generated and thus the more I/O activity required to perform a recovery operation.

The DBMS automatically recovers the data base and guarantees its integrity; it cannot guarantee that the programs generating the updates can be restarted. Each running program is responsible for participating in checkpoints only if it can be restarted. Transactions are typically coded to be brief, only interfacing with the checkpoint mechanism when they are finished. Unless large batch programs take checkpoints fairly often, large numbers of data base records could be locked for long periods. Therefore, these types of lengthy programs either should never be run simultaneously with online applications or must take internal snapshot checkpoints to synchronize their activities with the DBMS checkpoint. In this way a program can be restarted in the middle and remain consistent with the contents of the data base. This is usually accomplished by writing transaction-oriented batch programs that read a transaction and execute it to completion before reading the next transaction, thus allowing a checkpoint at the end of each transaction. Certain common coding techniques to optimize I/O efficiency in a batch program must be rewritten since no transaction should rely on any previous transaction. Moreover, such techniques as saving a record in case the next transaction needs it must be abandoned.

Another consideration during checkpoints is synchronizing the operation of the log tape(s) with the transaction controller, the DBMS, the operating system, and batch programs. This action prevents loss of transactions or processes. The specific software packages involved largely influence the outcome.

## Granularity

The simplest level of granularity used for the before and after images is identical to the physical unit of retrieval of a DBMS, called a block, or page. A single update causes one read of the desired page and one write each of a before image, an after image, and the modified page back to the disk (i.e., four I/O operations per update). Such a sequence can be initiated in some DBMSs by turning on a "must write" switch. This causes the update to be written to the data base when it occurs and is equivalent to a checkpoint. At this point, the before and after images can usually be written with one I/O operation.

Most systems attempt to reduce this overhead by employing some form of a least recently used (LRU) buffer management algorithm. LRU in a shared multibuffer environment is intended to keep active pages in the buffer while they are accessed. When a page is needed that is not currently in the buffer, the page in the buffer that has not been accessed for the longest time is replaced. If this page has been modified, an after image is first written to the log and the page written to the data base. Thus, a modified page is not written immediately but is held until space is needed for a successive read operation.

This technique is not without its drawbacks. In the case of the top level of inverted indexes, for example, pages could be held in memory for hours with hundreds of modifications that would not be represented in the data base. As a result, frequent checkpoints are mandatory—a checkpoint flushes all buffers (or at least those modified by a given program).

If page-level granularity is used, the recovery process involves overwriting pages in the data base without reading them first. If the after images are sorted into physical address order and reverse time sequence, only the most current after image of a given page must be written. This procedure significantly improves the roll-forward process; however, the cost of performing this sort select may exceed the savings realized. Although this process can also be applied to rollback, the usually brief time between checkpoints detracts from its cost-effectiveness.

Another technique that reduces throughput overhead uses record-level granularity to write before and after images. The advantage of this approach is that the size of the log file is greatly reduced, lessening the I/O activity to this file. The cost in system resources to write a single element of a full page is still one I/O operation, however. To use this technique optimally, the log is buffered (i.e., a block is not written until it contains enough updates, or images, to fill the buffer). Frequent checkpoints must again be performed.

Record-level granularity can cause fewer I/O operations to the log file. The recovery mechanism, however, is less efficient because the affected pages must be read, altered, and written back to the data base. All updates to a page—not just the most recent—must be performed. In situations where variable-length records are allowed, one record may occupy many pages during a processing period. This can complicate the location of the records, which must be modified if the updates (images) are applied in any order other than strict time sequence.

Another technique, item-level granularity (i.e., keeping track of how specific items were modified), can further reduce overhead during normal processing but can also delay recovery.

Another method involves keeping sufficient information to allow construction of the after image from the before image. A version of the transaction and indications of modified fields are stored. The advantage of this method is that a transaction that caused several pages to be modified can be contained in one log entry. Recovery is slower because the transactions must be processed from an intermediate phase, not the beginning. In addition, the log must be applied in strict time sequence to recover a data base from a restored copy.

## Recovery from Checkpoint Forward

The application of before and after images allows recovery from the time of the most recent checkpoint. Recovery can be extremely complicated, especially since multiple users could have simultaneously updated the same data. If the data base has been segregated into areas, each of which can be updated by only one user at a time, transactions completed since the last checkpoint can be rolled forward. This implies that during normal processing, other users were locked out of this area and possibly subjected to unacceptable delays. Incomplete transactions can be restored if a copy of the transaction was kept in the log.

If transactions are allowed to overlap (i.e., share data), the only roll-forward technique that can be used is reexecution of already completed transactions. For example, in Figure 6-1, Transaction B modifies Record 1. Transaction A then reads Record 1, using information in Record 1 to modify Record 2. Transaction A finishes normally, but the system fails before Transaction B completes. If Transaction A is recovered but not Transaction B, the data base is incorrect. In addition, the data base could have suffered structural damage if the information stored in Record 2 consisted of a pointer related to the information modified by Transaction B in Record 1. Transaction B alone cannot be recovered since it may contain within its own buffers structural information that was not contained on the log. A similar argument can be made about methods of rolling back selected instead of all transactions. The problem could be avoided with record locking, as Transaction A could not have read Record 1 until Transaction B released its lock.

Other mechanisms can solve this problem. For example, a checkpoint can be forced automatically when any transaction attempts to read a record (or page) modified by a different transaction since the last checkpoint. The bookkeeping activity, however, can be quite complicated and result in slow throughput.

The DBMS is responsible only for recovering the data. It is the responsibility of either the operations or programming staff to recover batch programs and of the teleprocessing monitor to recover transaction programs.

## Logging

The more log files generated, the more complex their synchronization. Alternatively, if only one comprehensive log file is generated, much recovery time is wasted skipping over information not needed by the recovery process. The basic trade-off is again between throughput and recovery efficiency.

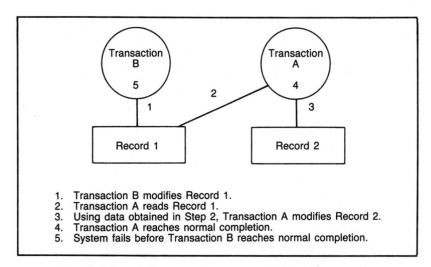

1. Transaction B modifies Record 1.
2. Transaction A reads Record 1.
3. Using data obtained in Step 2, Transaction A modifies Record 2.
4. Transaction A reaches normal completion.
5. System fails before Transaction B reaches normal completion.

**Figure 6-1. Recovery from Overlapping Transactions**

One technique for optimizing the log in the area of rollback is based on the assumption that the need to roll back beyond the most recent checkpoint will never arise. Accordingly, a separate, small disk file can be kept containing only the before images since the last checkpoint. When a checkpoint is taken, this file is simply repositioned at its starting point. This technique optimizes logging because before images are not kept on the main log tape(s). The speed of recovery is also enhanced because disk can be processed backward during recovery, eliminating the need to sort the before images.

Debate continues on whether tape or disk is better for log files. Tape is the popular medium because it is inexpensive and most installations can rarely spare disk space from online storage needs. Disk, however, is much faster and is usually considered more reliable than tape. It can be easily read backward or randomly, can be read simultaneously by more than one process, and can be spooled to tape later (possibly offline).

The log can never be allowed to run out of space. If a physical reel or device detects end of information, a scratch file must be instantly engaged to receive the information. This means that two drives or spindles must be dedicated to each log, four drives if dual logging is used for reliability. If disk logging is used, the log should never be on the same device as the data base.

## SYSTEM DESIGN CONSIDERATIONS

The recovery techniques discussed in this chapter are needed only in an environment that must support an online update capability. If no updates are performed during normal processing, there are no before or after images; recovery simply consists of turning the system back on or, at worst, running the restore utility with the most recent backup.

The system designer must first determine if the user can accept online edit/ validation of update transactions, with the actual transactions run later in a batch when the online system is disabled. This usually causes an overnight delay before updates are reflected in the file. The system designer should realize that the primary purpose of recovery is to assure the user that the system is reliable, accurate, and will not experience greater downtime than that specified by the user.

The basic user requirements necessary to establish appropriate strategies are acceptable downtime and the mean time between failures. The more important of the two is the former. Very short acceptable downtime is not always necessary. Users should be encouraged to establish realistic estimates to balance the trade-off between throughput and recovery time.

## SPECIAL ENVIRONMENTS

Any discussion of recovery should include distributed processing and the use of a back-end computer for all DBMS operations.

Recovery in a distributed environment can be complicated, depending on such factors as the extent of data sharing, the relative need for synchronization between computers, and the methods for resolving transactions on the same data from multiple sites. Recovery in distributed systems is beyond the scope of this chapter; it is mentioned merely to alert designers of recovery systems to the many problems they face.

A back-end computer affects recovery because all recovery mechanisms, other than the transaction log (and possibly even that), are handled completely by the back end. In addition, because a single back end can support multiple mainframes and multiple sets of users, a centralized recovery mechanism for all users must be achieved.

Careful examination of many current data base applications claiming almost perfect uptime reveals that they achieve this not with sophisticated recovery mechanisms but with duplicate hardware. Recovery was not considered an important topic in DP until the introduction of online update. Consequently, much work is needed before the technology is mastered, especially in environments requiring 24-hour uptime and very short acceptable downtime.

## CONCLUSION

Recovery must be considered an integral part of the system and data base design process. Systems analysts and data base designers must study the principles of restart and recovery and apply them throughout the design effort. Capabilities of the resident DBMS must be thoroughly understood before recovery tools can be effectively employed. Ultimately, the controlling factors are the user requirements for acceptable downtime and system throughput.

# 7 Concurrency in DBMSs

by John W. Young, Jr.

## INTRODUCTION

The problem of shared resources among concurrent processes predated the use of integrated data bases—operating systems have long been plagued by the problem. There are, however, fundamental differences between the features of an operating system and those of an integrated data base:

- A data base has vastly more shareable elements than an operating system; each record of the millions in a data base is potentially shareable on an individual basis, compared to the scores of components in an operating system.
- Changes in the sharing arrangement occur more frequently in a data base; each time a new record is requested, the pattern of sharing may change.
- The modes of sharing are more complex in a data base (e.g., a record data base may be read or written, or a number of data base records may be involved in a single operation).

An additional problem must be considered when studying problems of concurrency in a data base environment: an integrated data base must maintain its integrity and present a consistent view to all users at all times. The sharing of data among concurrent processes can adversely affect data base integrity and consistency.

Most solutions to the problem of concurrency involve some type of locking mechanism. With any of these, however, the problem of deadlock may occur. In fact, eliminating deadlocks is the root of the problem in resolving concurrency problems in data base management systems. The unique characteristics of data make many of the conventional solutions to deadlock difficult or impossible to apply.

This chapter investigates the problem of concurrency in light of its effect on data base integrity and consistency. Traditional solutions will be examined and some new ones presented.

## PROBLEMS OF CONCURRENCY

Data base integrity encompasses the accuracy, confidentiality, and reliability of data. The accuracy of data can be maintained through input validation, mechanisms to ensure that the data remains valid, and control of concurrent processes. Confidentiality can be ensured through access regulation, encryption, and other security controls. Finally, reliability of data can be maintained through hardware monitors, software monitors, and checkpoint and recovery procedures.

Consistency of data, the aspect of data base integrity that is addressed in this chapter, is a subset of the concept of accuracy of data. Maintaining consistency of data requires preventing semantic errors that may result from the interaction of two or more processes operating concurrently on a data base.

There are three major categories of inconsistencies that can be caused by uncontrolled concurrent processes. The following sections discuss how each can occur and how each affects data base integrity.

**Lost Updates.** This inconsistency is illustrated by the following example of uncontrolled concurrency between two transactions:

1. Transaction 1 (T1) reads record A.
2. T2 reads A.
3. T1 modifies the contents of A that it has read and rewrites them in the data base, erasing the original data read in Steps 1 and 2.
4. T2 modifies the contents of A that it read and rewrites them in the data base, erasing the modified version written by T1 in Step 3.

The effect of T1's update in Step 3 has been lost—if each transaction added one to the value of some field in A, a total of only one has been added to that field, not two as should have been the case.

**Reading of Inconsistent Data.** A simple example of this type of problem is the case in which T1 is reading sequentially by number through the customer account records and adding up the balances; other transactions, in particular T2, are updating the accounts. T1 reaches Account 500; at that point T2 transfers $1,000 from Account 002 to Account 998. That $1,000 will be counted twice by T1, once in each account, and an inconsistent result will be obtained. A similar situation would occur if T2 were inserting new accounts into the data base. T1 might process some of these accounts but not others (this is called the "phantom record" problem).

A variation of this problem would occur if T1 were reading account records at random and read Account 998 twice, once before the $1,000 was added and once after. This is referred to as an "unrepeatable read."

**Reading of Aborted Changes.** Suppose T1 adds $100,000 to Account 50 and T2 reads that new balance. Soon thereafter, T1 receives information (e.g., through the terminal operator depressing the VOID key) that the amount should have been $100. T1 can correct the value in the data base, but T2 will proceed with erroneous data.

A useful definition of data base consistency must acknowledge that each transaction is independent and should have an independent effect on the data base. With that in mind, the following definition of data base consistency is proposed:

> A data base is consistent after the execution of a group of concurrent transactions if its state is identical to what it would have been if the transactions had executed one after the other, in any order, without overlapping (i.e., each one finishing before the next started).

Since transactions occur randomly, their order is immaterial. If, for example, T1 transferred 10 teachers from the History to the Sociology department, and T2 gave all Sociology instructors a five percent raise, it is unknown and irrelevant whether those 10 teachers got the raise or not. What is important is that all of them did (T1 was followed by T2) or none of them did (T2 was followed by T1). The data base would be inconsistent if five instructors received raises and five did not—a state not corresponding to any sequence of nonoverlapped execution of T1 and T2. The transactions did not have independent effects.

## LOCKING

The solution to the problems of concurrency seems to be obvious. When two or more processes are operating on the same data in a potentially conflicting way, that data must be "locked" so that only a single process can operate on it at a time.

Two basic kinds of locks meet two different situations:

- A process (transaction) that is *reading* a data element holds a *shared* lock on it; this allows other concurrent processes to read it also (i.e., they can also hold shared locks on it) but prevents any concurrent process from updating the element.
- A process that is *writing* a data element holds an *exclusive* lock on it; this prevents any other process from either reading or writing it.

By applying the following rules, one can ensure that a data base will present a consistent view:

1. A process should get a shared lock on a data element before reading it.
2. A process should obtain an exclusive lock on a data element before writing it.
3. A shared lock on a data element will not be granted if anyone holds an exclusive lock on that element.
4. An exclusive lock on a data element will not be granted if anyone holds any lock on that element.
5. A process should hold a shared lock on a data element until it has completely finished reading that element.
6. A process should hold all of its exclusive locks until it has completed its

operations successfully and has finally written all modified data back into the data base.

Conscientious application of these rules will prevent the inconsistencies described earlier. The examples used to illustrate those inconsistencies can also show how the rules are applied:

- Lost updates—Since T1 is to update A, it obtains an exclusive lock on it. T2 cannot then access A until T1 is finished; T1's update is thus protected.
- Reading of inconsistent data—T1 obtained a shared lock on the whole set of customer accounts before starting to process it. T2, consequently, could not acquire an exclusive lock on the accounts it was to modify, nor could it insert new accounts. (The latter case could not be handled by locks on any existing records; rather, the record type "customer account" has to be locked against the insertion of any new instances.) In the example using customer record accounts stated earlier, T1 would have held a continuous shared lock on Account 998.
- Reading of aborted changes—According to rule 6, T2 could not have read the balance until after T1 had acknowledged the error and corrected it.

The use of the two kinds of locks, shared and exclusive, provides maximum concurrency for nonconflicting data base usages while protecting data base integrity and providing consistent views.

The discussion to this point has been entirely in terms of locking of logical entities (e.g., records). For implementation, however, it may be necessary to apply locks at the physical level (e.g., a sector on the disk is physically locked if any logical record on it is conceptually locked).

## GRANULARITY

A major decision affecting the performance of a data base system that uses locking is the size, or granularity, of the data grouping to be locked. If a transaction is to access a large number of records of the same type (or all of them), it may be more efficient to place a single lock on that record *type* rather than myriad locks on all record *instances*. The system designer must weigh the overhead of maintaining many locks against the loss in concurrency if a whole structure type is locked. For example, no other process could access any record of the locked type while the original transaction was in progress.

Ullman [1] proposes that the size of the lockable data group should be such that a transaction accesses a "few" elements. Thus, the element might be the record instance if the transaction were reading and writing individual instances, or the element might be the relation if the transaction were doing joins, selects, and the like on whole relations in a relational data base environment.

To provide a more flexible, efficient solution to the granularity problem, Gray and others [2] have developed a technique known as intention locking.

With this method the data types and instances are arranged in a hierarchy (e.g., data base, file, record type, record instances); the user can place a "warning" at any node in the hierarchy to signal that a descendant of that node is locked. This technique allows different transactions to manipulate different subtrees of the hierarchy without interference or excessive locking overhead, provided that their uses are mutually consistent.

## SPECIAL PROBLEMS AND SOLUTIONS

There are several problems on the issue of concurrency that require special solutions. These are discussed in the following sections.

### The Slow Reader

In a previous example, one process was reading sequentially through an entire section of the data base, while other processes were waiting to update that same section. If the section were left unlocked, the slow reader would not see a consistent view; if it were locked, however, the updating transactions might have to wait for a very long time. One solution to this dilemma is to lock that part of the data base long enough to make a fast copy of it—a snapshot—that the slow reader could use at its leisure. If the section is large, however, this solution may be impractical.

A faster but more complex alternative is to preserve a time-stamped copy of the old version of each record whenever it is modified during the time the slow reader is executing. When the slow reader gets to the point of the modification, it can look through the stack of record copies and, from the time stamps, determine the version that existed at the time it began execution. This allows any number of slow readers to operate on the same data simultaneously and independently. Of course, provision must be made for disposing of copies that no longer interest any slow reader.

### Temporary Inconsistency

If a set of integrity constraints has been specified for the data base, and if multistep transactions are being run against it, one or more of the integrity constraints may be temporarily violated between steps of the transaction. For example, a constraint may require that the total of the account balances be $1 million. This constraint will not be satisfied after a transaction has subtracted $1,000 from one account and before that figure is added to the intended account. Thus, a need exists for commands that suspend and resume the checking of integrity constraints.

### Levels of Consistency

The discussion so far has assumed that every transaction needs perfectly consistent views of the data base. IBM's System R, however, offers the interesting possibility of three levels of read consistency (total update consis-

tency is guaranteed by the system). These are:
- Level 1—One transaction may read changes made to the data base by another transaction before the latter has completed and has finally committed the modified data. Thus, the data read may later be disowned by the updating transaction.
- Level 2—Reads are not automatically reproducible (i.e., data read for a second time may not be identical to that in the first read), but protection against this can be requested by the transaction.
- Level 3—Full consistency is assured by the system.

This scheme allows more flexibility in balancing the needs of the application and transaction types against the overhead of concurrency control.

## Implicit versus Explicit Locking

In some systems, locking is implicit, controlled by whatever access command is issued to the DBMS (i.e., the DBMS will do whatever locking and unlocking is necessary to ensure data base consistency). In this mode, however, the DBMS has no way of knowing the user's intentions or requirements. As a result, the consistency control has to be on a "least common denominator" basis—the DBMS may be doing much more than is necessary. The user, however, is freed from the burden of worrying about concurrency problems.

In those systems that provide explicit locking, the user can fine tune concurrency control by locking only the required elements and by retaining the locks for as short a time as possible. This puts a serious responsibility on the user, however, since errors in the locking specification can damage data base integrity.

## Predicate Locks

In general, the locking techniques described depend on lock attachment to each element under consideration; that lock is turned on and off individually, depending on events in the system. If there is a large number of lockable elements (as is usually the case in a data base), the locking and unlocking overhead can become very large indeed. To overcome this problem, the concept of the predicate lock has been developed.

A predicate lock consists of a description or specification of the set of elements that should be locked on behalf of a particular operation; that is, it defines a logical predicate such that any element for which that predicate is true should be locked. Instead of having to manage thousands or millions of locks, the DBMS has only a (relatively) few predicate locks to administer.

To return to the example of the slow reader, suppose a summary were to be prepared for all customers in New York with balances of more than $1,000. Rather than locking all customer accounts, the predicate

LOCATION = 'NEW YORK' AND BALANCE > 1000

could be recorded. Whenever another process needs to update an account record, the predicate can be checked to see if that record is one that has been locked. An extension of the method checks a newly requested predicate lock to see if it conflicts with any existing one.

The high-level concept of predicate locks has several advantages over placing locks at the level of the object data. A predicate lock can specify the nonexistence of a record as well as its existence, thereby precluding the possibility of phantom records. The set of active locks is substantially smaller in a predicate locking scheme than in the analogous low-level locking scheme—the latter would have to lock each piece of data identified by the predicate. The predicate lock method results in less storage overhead for maintaining the lock list and fewer items to test for possible conflicts.

In theory, predicate locks provide the ideal means for both specifying and setting locks. In practice, severe problems appear when an attempt is made to identify the set of data specified by a complex predicate. In such situations the problem has proved to be recursively unsolvable. Therefore, the concept of predicate locks has centered around developing testing algorithms that will allow concurrent processing in the more common situations. These algorithms can be developed so that the degree of concurrency permitted can be traded off against the overhead costs associated with detecting nonobvious, "safe" processes.

Predicate locks must be considered superior to low-level locking mechanisms. Although the same amount of concurrency cannot be guaranteed, predicate locks will allow a reasonable amount of concurrency and will better ensure data base consistency.

## Data Base Locking in COBOL (CODASYL DML)

Data base locking in COBOL, the most popular programming language, deserves a special mention. When a data base record is accessed by a read-type operation, a select (shared) lock is established for it. That lock is maintained as long as the record is in use (i.e., for a run unit, set type, record type, or realm) and prevents any other run unit from executing a write-type operation against it.

When a record is accessed by a write-type operation (including FIND FOR UPDATE), an update (exclusive) lock is established. That lock is maintained until the end of the run unit or until the run unit executes a COMMIT statement. The lock prevents any other access to the record. In COBOL, updated versions of data base records are not made available immediately to other run units. Rather, they are held in abeyance until the run unit performs a COMMIT, at which time the modifications are made in the data base and are available to other run units.

Since a program may be instructed to preserve the contents of several records read during its execution, even after they are no longer in use, the user may define a named keep list. While a record is still current for a run unit (and therefore shared locked), the program may give a "KEEP keep-list-name" command that will place the record's data base key at the top of the designated keep list. In addition to the currency indicator criterion, a record will now remain shared locked as long as it appears on any keep list. It may be removed from a keep list by a FREE command. All keep lists are emptied by a COMMIT or at the end of the run unit.

CODASYL DML also has concurrency control at the realm level—the READY (open) statement can specify that a shared or exclusive lock be applied to the designated realm(s). It persists until a FINISH (close) statement or the end of the run unit is reached.

## Reaction to a Lock

A system may take either of two approaches when a process tries to access a locked record in a prohibited mode (e.g., tries to modify a record that is shared locked):

- A status may be returned to the process and indicate that it has attempted to violate a lock restriction. The process may then continue its execution and try the operation later. Eventually, of course, it may have to go into a loop, repetitively trying the command until it is successful.
- The process may be suspended and entered in a queue to await record availability, when it is then reactivated.

In some systems, the requestor may specify which of these methods is desired.

## DEADLOCK

The simplest kind of deadlock is shown by the following example:
1. Process A exclusive-locks resource X.
2. Process B exclusive-locks resource Y.
3. Process A tries to lock resource Y and waits.
4. Process B tries to lock resource X and waits.

A is waiting for B to release Y, which B cannot do because B is waiting for A to release X. Neither process can proceed further, and deadlock results.

Deadlock can occur only when all of the following five conditions exist:
- Concurrency—Two or more processes simultaneously compete for exclusive use of two or more sets of data.
- Locking—A process can be given exclusive use of data.
- Additional locking—A process can request additional locks while holding locks to other sets of data.
- No preemption—A set of data cannot be forcibly taken (preempted) from a process that has locked that data.
- Circular wait—A circular chain of processes exists such that each process locks a set of data that is being requested by the next process in the chain.

The problem of deadlock can be averted by avoiding any one of these conditions.

## Solving Deadlock

There are four basic methodologies proposed for handling deadlock. A brief discussion of each follows.

**Ignoring Deadlock.** This could be called the nonsolution. No mechanisms for solving the problems of deadlock are built into the system. When a deadlock occurs, it must be detected by some external means (e.g., telling an operator or affected user that a process has been waiting for a time longer than some threshold). At that time, one of the deadlocked processes could be terminated through external means. Of course, if any updates had been completed by the terminated process, they would have to be backed out (undone) in order to preserve data base consistency. More crucial to this discussion are the intolerable delays that such a strategy would cause—deadlocks in a data base system are more frequent than in an operating system. Ignoring deadlocks is counterproductive.

**Detecting Deadlock and Backing Out.** In the example of deadlock given, the deadlock could be detected when process B requests the data that process A has already locked, thus completing a cycle. The policy of deadlock detection and backout requires a mechanism that can detect when a deadlock has occurred. This entails using a "state graph" that indicates the status of the data base relative to the interactions of the active processes and data at a particular time. The state graph is updated whenever a process becomes active or terminates and whenever a granule of data is allocated or released. This graph is examined for a chain of locks, implying a deadlock (circular wait), whenever a process has to wait (or possibly periodically at longer intervals).

Once the deadlock has been detected, the more complex problem of backout must be addressed. There are at least two approaches. The first requires the termination of one or more of the deadlocked processes, and the second involves the preemption of data from one or more of the deadlocked processes. In either case, it may prove desirable to use another algorithm whose function would be to determine the optimal backout process that would alleviate the deadlock condition. In general, this will be the backout process whose cost is least.

Since backout costs can be high, techniques for accelerating backout should be considered (e.g., having a process do its updating on a copy of the relevant portion of the data base). If the process terminates successfully, pointers are changed to incorporate the copy into the data base, simultaneously removing the original from it. If backout is needed, the original is simply left in place.

**Avoiding Deadlock.** Avoiding deadlock requires advance information on the data requirements of a process. The basic approach is to alleviate the additional locking condition by not allowing a process to proceed until safe. As with deadlock detection, avoiding deadlock requires a state graph and the associated manipulation algorithms.

In order to avoid deadlock, the DBMS must examine the data requirements of the process in question and determine if the request is safe. An unsafe process is placed in a wait queue. When an active process releases its set of data, all processes on the wait queue are reexamined for safety. Thus, in addition to the overhead costs associated with maintaining state graphs, avoidance can cause a process to become permanently blocked. This drawback could be overcome by attaching a counter to each process that would indicate the number of times the process has been examined for safety. When the counter reaches some threshold, no new process would be allowed to lock data that the blocked process requires. Eventually, the active process causing the delay would terminate, and the blocked process could continue.

In a low-level locking scheme, the a priori specification of required data is impossible because access may be required to a set of data whose values indicate a subsequent set of needed data. The strategy of avoidance, then, could not be utilized by such low-level locking schemes. A high-level predicate locking scheme, however, could use the strategy of avoiding deadlocks because the predicates provide a mechanism for stating the data requirements a priori. Also, the state graphs and associated algorithms would no longer be needed in a predicate locking scheme. Instead, the DBMS would examine the predicates for possible conflicts and only grant the safe requests. This is another argument for using predicate locks.

**Preventing Deadlock.** Deadlock can occur only if all five conditions exist—concurrency, locking, additional locking, no preemption, and circular wait. If one or more of those conditions could be obviated, deadlock could be prevented. The prevention of deadlock can be accomplished through one of four basic mechanisms: presequencing, preordering, preemption, or preclaiming.

Reviewing the conditions for deadlock reveals that the locking condition cannot be overcome without sacrificing data base consistency. The condition of concurrency could be relieved through the mechanism of presequencing, which entails the ordering of processes to execute serially. Although this would solve all problems of concurrency, it would lead to an intolerable level of inefficiency.

Preordering can prevent the condition of circular wait. This technique requires that each data granule be ordered in some manner and that requests for data granules follow the given ordering. Thus, a circular chain of data requests could not occur, and deadlock would be prevented. Unfortunately, the characteristics of data make such a strategy difficult to implement. The major pitfalls of preordering are the need for a means to present the ordering of data granules to all users, the lack of data independence, and the impractical restriction that the user access data in the specified order.

Another condition for deadlock specifies that no preemption be allowed. The obvious solution to this condition would be to allow preemption. When the possibility of a deadlock has been detected, the preemption of needed data resources could prevent the deadlock from occurring; however, the preemption of data from a process that has already begun to operate upon that data would require backing out its changes.

The final condition for deadlock, that of allowing additional locking, can be relieved by requiring that each process start out by requesting all of its data at one time (the preclaim strategy). This is difficult, however, since the first data accessed may determine what data will be needed later.

Another implementation involves breaking down processes into a series of subprocesses, each with its own data requirements. At the beginning of each subprocess, the required data is locked; at the end of each subprocess, all data is released. This technique requires that the processes be broken down in such a manner that data base consistency and process integrity are preserved.

In all variations of the preclaim strategy, one restriction must be noted. Never is a sequence of events allowed whereby a process locks data, modifies the data, and then requests that additional data sets be locked.

The preclaim strategy is similar to the strategy for avoiding deadlock. The distinction lies in that to avoid deadlock, a process is not allowed to proceed until a safe state can be guaranteed; the preclaim strategy requires that a process set all necessary locks before being allowed to proceed. The problem of a process becoming permanently blocked also exists under the preclaim strategy and can be solved through the same countermechanism used to avoid deadlock (attaching counters to each process).

For high-level locks, the preclaim strategy is identical to the strategy described for avoiding deadlock. Of all strategies for preventing deadlock, preclaim is the only one that is feasible in a data base environment.

## CONCLUSION

Concurrent processes must be controlled in order to maintain process integrity and data base integrity and consistency. Any mechanism for controlling concurrent processes should have certain features:

- The mechanism should be able to maintain the consistency of the data base, despite the actions of a process.
- The mechanism should not depend upon external means (e.g., operator interference or prescheduling of processes).
- The mechanism should not allow a process to become permanently blocked in order to prevent a possible deadlock or as a result of a deadlock.
- The mechanism should allow locking at a level of granularity that is sufficiently fine to provide reasonable efficiency.

In addition, the mechanism should separate the user from the problems of concurrency. The user should not be responsible for data integrity threatened by the interaction of concurrent processes; nor should the user be concerned with the other processes that are executing simultaneously with his.

One of the best mechanisms for specifying and setting locks is predicate locking. Such a high-level locking scheme sets logical locks that eliminate the problem of phantom records.

Unfortunately, any locking mechanism is faced with the possibility of dead-locks. Of the several approaches to solving the deadlock issue, only detection and backout, avoidance, and preclaiming are feasible. It is not yet clear which of these is optimal.

#### References

1. Ullman, J. *Principles of Database Systems*, Potomac MD: Computer Science Press, 1980.
2. Gray, J.N., Putzolu, F., and Traiger, I. "Granularity of Locks and Degrees of Consistency in a Shared Data Base." *Modeling in Data Base Management Systems*, Amsterdam: North-Holland, 1976, 365–394.

#### Bibliography

Date, C.J. *An Introduction to Database Systems*, 2nd ed. Reading MA: Addison-Wesley, 1977.

Eswaren, K. P., et al. "On the Notions of Consistency and Predicate Locks." *Communications of the ACM*, Vol. 19, No. 1 (November 1976), 624–633.

Gray, J.N. "Notes on Data Base Operating Systems," *Operating Systems—An Advanced Course*, Edited by P. Bayer, et al. New York: Springer-Verlag, 1978, 393–481.

Potier, D., and Leblanc, Ph. "Analysis of Locking Policies in Database Management Systems," *Communications of the ACM*, Vol. 23, No. 10 (October 1980), 584–593.

Ries, D.R., and Stonebraker, M.R. "Effects of Locking Granularity in a Data Base Management System," *ACM Transactions Data Base Systems*, Vol. 2, No. 3 (September 1977), 233–246.

Ries, D.R. and Stonebraker, M.R. "Locking Granularity Revisited," *ACM Transactions Data Base Systems*, Vol. 4, No. 2 (June 1979), 210–227.

Schiao, K., and Ozsu, T.M. *A Survey of Concurrency Control Mechanisms for Centralized and Distributed Data Bases*. Ohio State University Computer and Information Science Research Center, OSU-CISRC-TR-81-1, February 1981.

Stonebraker, M. and Wong, E. "Access Control in a Relational Data Base Management System by Query Modification." *Proceedings 1977 ACM Annual Conference*, 180–186.

Yannakakis, M., Papadimitriou, C.H., and Kung, H.T. "Locking Policies: Safety and Freedom from Deadlock." IEEE. *Proceedings 20th Annual Symposium Foundations of Computer Science*, 1979, 286–297.

# ⑧ Administration of Data Bases in a Distributed Environment    by Bernard K. Plagman

## INTRODUCTION

Data bases are generally viewed as centralized, with all data residing physically in one location under the control of the data base management system (DBMS). Control over a centralized environment is typically an administrative function, which includes responsibility over the entire spectrum of the data resource. This type of control helps ensure the integrity of data that is shared by a number of applications and users.

In the distributed data base environment, coordination and control are required among users and programs in physically dispersed locations. Thus, it may not be desirable, or even possible, for a centralized control group to perform the data/data base administration (DA/DBA) functions that generally must be performed in more than one location.

Distribution of data tends to weaken DBMS data integrity mechanisms. The identical data base concept that when implemented in a centralized environment brings increased control tends to reduce control in a distributed environment. Furthermore, distribution of data tends to be most applicable in organizations with autonomous, decentralized management. This type of management structure is not conducive to the implementation of a centralized data administration activity.

The goal is to find an effective balance between the decentralized processing and management of data, on the one hand, and the need for centralized coordination and control of the data resource on the other. This chapter discusses data/data base administration in a distributed data base environment. The terms used are defined in the following paragraphs.

**Data Base Administration.** Data base administration is primarily a technical function. Its roots are in the systems programming and applications development fields, and its evolving role combines aspects of both. Its purpose is highly specialized and wedded to the maintenance of the DBMS software, the data base files, and the applications that maintain and access the data base files. The DBA is assigned complete responsibility for and authority over the data base files, their design and integrity, and the specification and management of related ancillary utility functions through the entire application life cycle. In this way, all technical and implementation problems can be addressed. Because the DBA role is tied to the DBMS and its facility, it is site oriented.

**Data Administration.** Although data administration includes all data base administration functions, there are some differences. Whereas the DBA role is traditionally limited to those applications and files using the DBMS, data administration encompasses all data in an organization. The DA's job is usually more conceptual, less technical, and exists at a higher level within the organization than that of the DBA. In many organizations with a DA function, the DBA group is subordinate to that function. The DA is more oriented to users and their business needs than is the DBA, whose users are within the DP area and whose concerns are more technical. Figure 8-1 shows a typical data and data base administration organizational relationship.

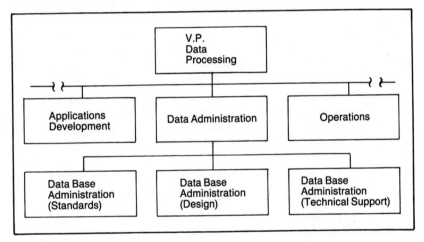

**Figure 8-1. Relationship of Data Base Administration to Data Administration**

**Distributed Processing.** Distributed processing, generally speaking, is the placement of some or all of the following DP functions at physically dispersed locations:
- Data entry
- Data manipulation
- Data storage
- Data retrieval
- Data display

These locations (nodes) are linked by a telecommunications network.

**Distributed Data Base.** CODASYL defines data base environment as one that includes a data base, a DBMS, a data base definition (schema), and a user schema. Placing data base management functions at one or more locations in a distributed processing environment produces a distributed data base environment.

To be effective, a DBMS must control all data base activity. In fact, the one characteristic that generally differentiates a data base environment from a non-data-base environment is that, in the former, all data file activity is handled and coordinated through a DBMS.

In a distributed data base environment (see Figure 8-2), whether the data bases are partitioned or replicated, the DBMS functions must be performed as if the data at the dispersed locations were logically one integrated unit. This implies the ability to organize, control, and provide access to data base data wherever it is located and to maintain its integrity regardless of how or by whom it is updated. The mechanics of data location and integrity maintenance are handled by the network data base management system (NDBMS).

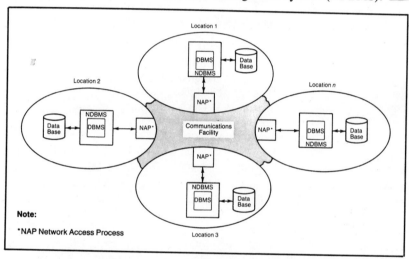

Figure 8-2. Distributed Data Base Environment

**Distributed Administration of Data.** In a distributed data base environment, the DA/DBA function controls, designs, and defines the data base from an administrative viewpoint. The geographically dispersed (local) administration functions are handled by local DA/DBAs whose activities should be coordinated across the network (see Figure 8-3).

## SYSTEMS DEVELOPMENT AND DATA BASE DESIGN CONSIDERATIONS

Each distributed data base location is autonomous and under the control of a local designer, who addresses local problems. Taken together, there is a multiplicity of activity that, unless coordinated or controlled, leads to incompatability of design methodology and design and thus to complications in the interlocation communications process.

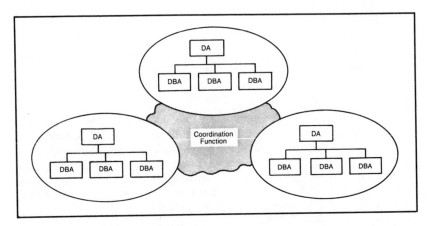

Figure 8-3. Distributed Data/Data Base Administration Environment

Between any two nodes there is a single interface; however, as nodes are added to the network, the interfaces proliferate (see Figure 8-4). Resolution of access and update among nodes is handled by the NDBMS. The NDBMS represents the functions, over and above those of the DBMS, that are necessary to support internodal use of data. The NDBMS must provide support for each of the following possibilities for each data base file:

- A partitioned data base, with pieces stored at different nodes
- A replicated data base, with multiple copies stored at multiple nodes
- A combination of replicated and partitioned data bases

Although it may be technically feasible to provide an NDBMS to support such distribution, the coordination function becomes increasingly complex. Because of changing local needs, the *modi operandi* of nodes tend to drift further and further apart. Should that evolution proceed unchecked, it could negate the distributed data base environment and supplant it with a group of totally autonomous data base environments. If distribution of function is to be effective, this evolutionary drift must be controlled.

## Alternative Strategies and Guidelines

To control this drifting and to provide a basis for communication among nodes, a DA/DBA equivalent of the NDBMS should be created. This function would provide the organizational interface mechanism between the local DA/DBA groups. This interface function should address the areas indicated in the following sections.

**A Common or Standard Systems Development Life Cycle (SDLC).** This provides the mechanism for a common development interface and identifies those points at which distributed data base considerations must be addressed from a global viewpoint. In addition, an SDLC should provide a common method of documentation that can promote better internodal communication.

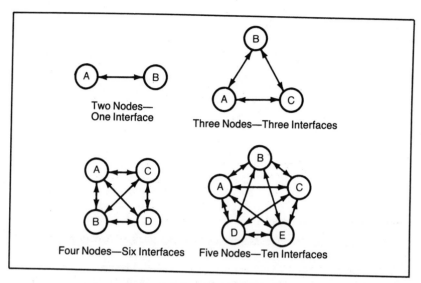

**Figure 8-4. Interface Multiplication**

**Data Base Design Methodology.** The coordinating DBA uses the data base design methodology to distribute and coordinate the data base design efforts at each location in much the same way as the DBA controls the integration of data base design at a single location. This centralized function has primary, or at least coordinative, responsibility for the design of interfaces among nodes in the distributed environment and primary control over data changes in all locations. In addition, this function addresses problems of integrity and design or definitional changes that occur at one node and are also needed at other nodes. The local DA/DBA handles any intralocation design efforts.

In addition, a common design methodology for data bases in a distributed environment can help ensure that distribution alternatives for data are considered, based on a set of commonly understood and accepted design criteria. This topic is discussed later in this chapter.

**The Data Dictionary/Directory System (DD/DS).** The DD/DS in a distributed environment can be divided into central and local functions. The central DD/DS would maintain definitional and locater information on all distributed data. The local DD/DS would maintain the local metadata and transmit through the central DD/DS those changes that should be propagated through the network. The central DD/DS in a distributed environment may contain many variants of metadata as a result of the local evolutionary process. It acts as the catalyst for data translation whenever data is transferred from one location to another and incompatibility is recognized. Update control and the total definition of the data bases are maintained through the DD/DS.

## The Design of Distributed Data Bases

Only from a global vantage point can the following distributed data base decisions be made:
- To distribute or maintain data bases centrally
- To replicate or partition data bases
- To distribute the DD/DS or maintain it centrally (or some combination thereof)
- To determine who has what responsibility and authority

These distribution decisions must be made centrally to ensure maximum global-level balance in performance and integrity. Nonetheless, each decision has an impact on each node. Thus, although processing of the distributed data is performed locally and responsibility for this processing resides locally, distribution decisions should be made centrally.

This dilemma is further complicated by the desire of local personnel to design their own data bases. The issue is where the distribution decision making should end and local data base design should begin. While managers at local nodes may have been led to believe the distribution of data would lead to greater autonomy in decision making, the centrally made distribution decisions may be more constraining than anticipated. The solution to this difficulty is the specification and use of a carefully procedurized data base design methodology for distributed data bases.

As the technology of distributed data bases evolves, this decision-making dilemma could worsen. Consider, for example, when the NDBMS and DD/DS allow dynamic replication and partitioning of data bases, contingent on access patterns and processing requirements. This movement and placement of data must be controlled. Heavy reliance on the NDBMS and the DD/DS to maintain the distributed network must be closely coordinated with DA/DBA design activities at the nodes to ensure compatibility among nodes.

The complexity of the environment requires more technical expertise on the part of the designers and greater administrative control on the part of the respective DA/DBA staffs. More emphasis must be placed on the higher-level conceptual design efforts that will coordinate activities across nodes. Related SDLC standards must be created.

The designer can no longer address the local environment in isolation. He or she must be aware of the environment beyond the interface. The local node is part of a whole; it is both dependent on and independent of the whole. Recognizing this, the designer must examine the impact of all design decisions beyond the immediate local environment.

## OPERATIONS AND PRODUCTION CONSIDERATIONS

The distributed data base environment poses additional operational and production considerations that the DA/DBA charged with the control and coordination of the environment must address. The solutions are administrative in nature. Although technical implementation features are a part of the

NDBMS facilities, the DA/DBA is responsible for specifying parameters and procedures that properly govern production.

## Administration and Control

Whether there are few or many locations or few or many DBMSs in the distributed environment, procedures must enable a coordinated and integrated functioning of the entire data base network. These procedures must ensure that all locations are synchronized from the data base point of view as well as from the viewpoints of the dictionaries, directories, operations, and documentation. In addition, because of the heavy dependence on data base software, all version and release updates must be coordinated and propagated through the network on a timely basis.

The control and coordination procedures must extend through the maintenance of application programs that process the data base. Procedures for applying changes must be reflected in all components.

## Restart and Recovery Considerations

The greater complexity of restart and recovery in the distributed environment is caused by both the necessity to synchronize the process across nodes and by a correspondingly greater number of recovery options. Operational procedures must be carefully established, taking into account the coordination and synchronization of recovery activities at each node in the network. All nodes must be able to recover to the same point in time. This is difficult because of computer clock synchronization; it is even more difficult when the operational schedules of the nodes differ because of location in different time zones.

Each possible type of location or network failure must be identified and analyzed. The state of the data at each node must be accurately determined as a precondition to each recovery operation.

Unlike the centralized data base environment in which the recovery operation is either successful or not, it is conceivable that in a distributed environment some nodal recoveries may succeed, while others fail. Sufficient backup must be maintained to ensure that recovery can be achieved at all nodes and that individual nodes can continue processing despite failures at other nodes. Partitioned data bases must be examined after recovery to ensure that the node-to-node linkages are all intact. Replicated data bases must be compared to ensure synchronization or must be redistributed if possible.

Because distributed data bases are physically separate but logically connected and data location is transparent to the end user, failure at one location may affect other locations. It may be difficult, however, to determine quickly exactly where the data base physically failed when irregularities are reported by end users. Note that local recovery procedures should include global user notification, just as local recovery includes global verification and validation.

## Access Control Considerations

The DBMS operating on individual nodes of a network provides intranodal security requirements in much the same way as a central-site DBMS provides data base security needs. The administration of the access control mechanism of the NDBMS relates to the specification of security profiles that span nodes on the network. The major consideration involves authorization of a process initiated at one node to access data at another. This procedure is referred to as delegation.

In a distributed environment in which internodal data access is transparent to the user, the security profile must be carefully specified and maintained by the DA/DBA to ensure that the transfer of data and requests from one node to another does not result in unauthorized access of data. This can only be accomplished with a global view of the network and its distributed data base design. Maintenance of the distributed security profile must also be centrally coordinated by the DA/DBA; a change to security profiles must not adversely affect processing patterns or allow inadvertent delegation of authority to access data at another node.

Access control for the distributed data base environment is not only a data base technology issue; communications technology can and should also provide for the implementation of security needs. Access control to executing processes, operational terminals, and/or lines should augment the access control mechanism implemented in the DBMS and the NDBMS. Data in transmission can also be encrypted. It is the responsibility of the DA/DBA to coordinate these activities on an ongoing basis.

## ORGANIZATIONAL ISSUES

Those organizations that have migrated to a distributed processing environment have found effective DP strategies in support of decentralized management. Control of development and operations is thus passed to local sites. The trends toward autonomy, as evidenced by user organizational structures, extend to the DP departments that service those structures.

Simultaneously, these same organizations have started to use data base technology for their application systems—one of the strongest centralization forces in DP today. This paradox of centralization because of data base as opposed to decentralization as a result of distribution must be addressed by management and data/data base administrators, who must resolve the inherent conflict between their data base needs and the needs of the distributed processing environment.

### An Alternative Strategy

A division of functions, some local and some global, has resulted as the role of the DA/DBA in a distributed environment has evolved. The global (network-wide) functions are organization-wide and thus corporate in nature. The local functions fall within the domain of local management.

One way to handle this situation is to divide responsibilities along the lines of the distributed processing itself (see Figures 8-5 and 8-6). That is, the local DA/DBA function, which must operate within the guidelines and procedures specified by the corporate DA/DBA, would deal with local development and operations. The strictly local portions of the data base would, of course, be fully controlled locally.

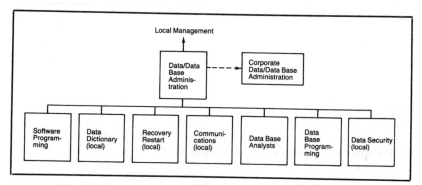

**Figure 8-5. Local Data/Data Base Administration Organization**

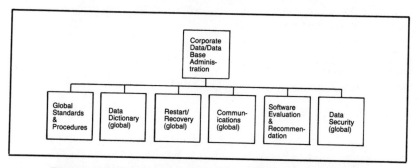

**Figure 8-6. Corporate Data/Data Base Administration Organization**

The corporate DA/DBA functions would address network maintenance and the data communications aspect of internodal data base access. The corporate DA/DBA would have primary responsibility for planning and coordinating global recovery (including problem extent determination), recovery scheduling, and global validation after recovery. The actual recovery operations would be executed and handled at the affected nodes. In addition, the corporate unit would have overall responsibility to coordinate network change control, with documentation maintenance to ensure that all nodes receive change information. They would also resolve conflicts among nodes as they pertain to data base use and modification. The corporate unit would also have to make DBMS software decisions that maintain the global compatibility of the data base environment.

There are many potential political conflicts between corporate and local functions. The autonomy intended by the distribution of processing is partially negated by the requirements of the data base environment. This conflict must be well understood and resolved.

## CONCLUSION

The distributed data base environment must evolve; it cannot be imposed. Before attempting migration from a centralized organization, there should be careful planning. Before implementation, procedures, standards, and controls must be developed, accepted by all parties, and tested. Local and corporate management responsibilities must be clearly delineated.

In addition, all DA/DBA staff members must thoroughly understand the environment. Extensive training may be required to provide technical and conceptual understanding at all levels.

**Bibliography**

Canning, R.G. "Distributed Data Systems." *EDP Analyzer.* Vol. 14, No. 7 (June 1976).

Canning, R.G. "Network Structures for Distributed Systems." *EDP Analyzer,* Vol. 14, No. 7 (July 1976).

Cashing, P.G. "Data Base Interworking." *Network Systems and Software.* Maidenhead, England: Infotech International Ltd., 1975.

Comba, P.G. "Needed: Distributed Control." *Proceedings of the International Conference on Very Large Data Bases.* New York NY: Association for Computing Machinery, 1975.

Davis, G.B. *Management Information Systems.* New York: McGraw-Hill, 1974.

Lowenthal, Eugene I. "The Distributed Data Management Function." *Proceedings of the National Computer Conference.* Montvale NJ: AFIPS Press, 1974.

"The Data Base Administrator." GUIDE Information Management Group, November 1972.

# ⑨ Distributed Data Bases on Unlike Computers

by Grayce Booth

## INTRODUCTION

A distributed data base exists when related data elements are stored at two or more processors within a distributed system. When applied to the elements of a distributed data base, the term related is quite flexible; the relationship can be either very close and require a great deal of coordination among the processors or can be very loose and require only minimal coordination. In any case, the existence of this relationship distinguishes a distributed data base from multiple independent data bases.

Distributed data bases can be partitioned or replicated. A partitioned data base exists when each part or segment contains unique data elements. Alternatively, the segments can contain partially or entirely redundant data elements, forming a replicated data base. Combinations of partitioning and replication are also possible.[1]

### Unlike Computers

When the need arises to expand a centralized system, an organization is likely to acquire a number of minicomputers, place them in point-of-transaction locations, and distribute some of the processing and data base(s) to those locations. Often there are good business and/or technical reasons for acquiring the minis from someone other than the mainframe vendor; in such situations the probability of differences between the minis and the mainframe is great. Even if the minicomputers are from the vendor who supplied the central processor, they may be incompatible with that computer. Therefore, a hierarchically distributed system [2] (see Figure 9-1) involves some degree of difference between the host processor and the satellite processors.

A distributed data base can involve different kinds of computers when two previously independent processors are linked to form a distributed system. These computers may have served different divisions or departments or even different companies now combined through merger or acquisition. Because each system was selected by a different organization and, perhaps, for different uses, the type of computer may differ in each case. The result is a horizontally distributed system [2] (see Figure 9-2).

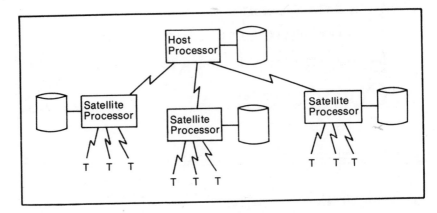

Figure 9-1. Hierarchically Distributed System

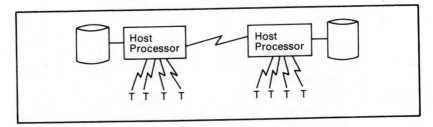

Figure 9-2. Horizontally Distributed System

This type of system might also be used because a single organizational entity requires two or more types of computers for different purposes. For example, a specialized scientific processor and a specialized time-sharing processor might be used in an engineering organization. These computers might require access to common data; in that case, a distributed data base would be established to provide shared data access.

A major technical challenge associated with the use of distributed data bases is how to provide access to remotely stored data. For example, how can a user whose terminal is attached to one processor obtain data stored at another? The same problem exists when a program executing (or submitted for execution) at one processor needs data stored at another processor. The remote-access problem can be solved by program migration (moving the program to the data) and data migration (moving the data to the program). This chapter describes the methods of locating data elements, the two remote-access strategies, the various differences that may be encountered, how these differences affect the access strategy chosen, and how to resolve (or avoid) the problems in each case. To simplify the discussion, the following sections assume that only two computers are involved (the same situations would exist regardless of the number of computers in the distributed system).

## LOCATING DATA ELEMENTS

When a terminal user or an application program requires access to data elements that are part of a distributed data base, logic must be provided to determine where the required elements are stored, regardless of whether the program or the data will be moved to provide access. Much or all of this logic is either included in the application programs or supplied by the terminal users. In the longer term, the logic will move into the system software, using one or more of the methods outlined.

### The Schema

In the CODASYL approach to data bases (and in most modern data base software systems), a description of the data base structure and formats is stored with the data base (rather than in the accessing programs). This description is called a schema.

In a schema-based DBMS, each access to the data base is interpretive, and the schema is used to determine how to accomplish each access (see Figure 9-3).

A distributed data base can be described by a global schema that defines all elements and relationships of the entire data base. If the global schema is stored at each computer within the distributed system, access requests can be mapped against it, regardless of where the requested data element(s) is stored.

There is no reason why a single global schema cannot describe data base segments with different data structures. In fact, the Honeywell implementation of the CODASYL recommendations, Integrated Data Store/II (IDS/II), allows a single schema to describe indexed and network/hierarchical structures as part of one data base. The only restriction is that indexed structures and network/hierarchical structures must be in different areas of the data base. Area is a concept that allows the data base administrator (DBA) to separate the logical data base into subdivisions to be mapped independently onto physical storage. In fact, the area concept can be easily extended to the distributed data base environment.

Conceptually, a distributed data base is a single logical data base, segments of which are partitioned and/or replicated and associated with two or more computers. For the long-term development of a distributed DBMS, the use of global schemas and the association of one or more areas with each computer seems logical.

The use of the global schema can be considered if each computer in the distributed system supports a schema-based DBMS. The schema at each location can describe local and remote area(s), although the local DBMS will not have access to the remote data. Of course, differences in data formats and/or structures must be considered when attempting to set up a global schema; and if the differences are significant, schema use may be impractical. If feasible, however, this approach allows compilation of applications and/or end-user procedures that access local as well as remote data elements.

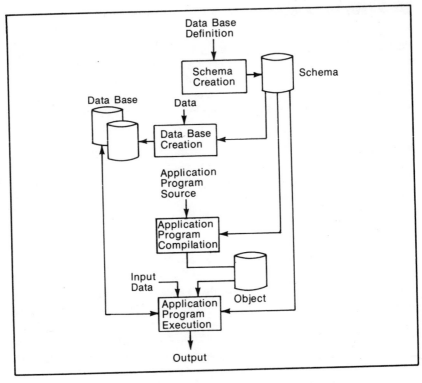

**Figure 9-3. Schema-Based Data Base Management**

## Catalogs

Data elements in a distributed data base can also be located by using catalogs to indicate where specific data sets are stored. Catalogs usually maintain information at the data set, file, or area level rather than at the data element level as schemas do.

A global catalog can list remotely accessed data sets, indicating where each resides. If a copy of the global catalog is maintained at each computer, the location of all globally accessible data elements can always be determined. The main difficulty with this approach is that all copies of the global catalog must be kept current (this same problem applies to global schemas). In practice, however, catalog updates will probably occur infrequently, thus minimizing the difficulty of keeping all copies synchronized.

It may be practical to extend an existing catalog facility so that it can perform global catalog functions. If this can be done, the amount of data-location logic required in application programs and/or in terminal user procedures will be minimized.

## Data Dictionary

The use of a global data dictionary is another way to keep track of data elements in a distributed data base. A data dictionary serves many of the same purposes as does a schema in describing the data base structure and formats and also supplies "where used" information (i.e., which application(s) uses each data element). The data dictionary, however, is a DBA aid that is used to manage data base content and use, while the schema is used directly by the DBMS software to access the data base.

A good data dictionary system can probably accommodate descriptions for both local and remote data elements; thus, the distributed data base and its use can be controlled through the single data dictionary. Unlike the global schema and global catalog, the data dictionary does not automate the process of dynamically finding data in a distributed data base. A single data dictionary, however, can assist the DBA in overall management of that data base.

## PROGRAM MIGRATION

In a distributed system, a terminal user or an application program associated with one computer may require access to distributed data base elements associated with another. As shown in Figure 9-4, a user at terminal A1 can easily be provided with access to data base segment A. If, however, the user requires access to data base segment B, the situation is more complex. One way to provide the needed access is through program migration. In program migration, the data base access program is sent and executed where the required data element(s) resides, and some or all of the output produced is then returned to the other location.

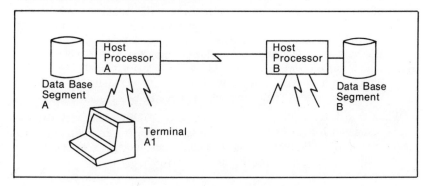

**Figure 9-4. Access to Remote Data**

## Object or Source Migration

Program migration between computers can occur in object or source form. If the program is sent in object form, it can be placed in execution immediately upon receipt. If sent in source form, the program must be compiled before being executed.

The degree of difference between computers affects program migration. It is often difficult to move a program in object form between unlike computers. If host A supports a cross-compiler for host B, it can generate object code suitable for that system, allowing object-form program migration between unlike computers.

Of course, object-code compatibility is only one of the points to be considered. In many computers a program requires such further processing as linking to library routines and/or editing for correct loading format before it is ready for execution. If the target computer (the one on which the moved program is to be executed) requires this type of program preparation, it must be provided either before or after program migration.

Movement of the program in source rather than object form decreases compatibility problems because source programs are more likely to be compatible than are object programs. Complete compatibility, however, cannot be assumed and must be planned for carefully.

In assessing program compatibility, it is important to ensure that capabilities with the same name are, in fact, identical. For example, the fact that most computers support COBOL does not guarantee compatibility and transferability for COBOL programs.

The industry-standard definition of COBOL is updated periodically, and a specific computer may or may not support the most recent version. In addition, COBOL is defined in terms of a language nucleus plus a series of modules (e.g., table handling, sequential I/O, sort/merge). The nucleus consists of a low-level portion that provides basic internal operations and a high-level portion for more extensive options. Some of the language modules also have low and high options. Therefore, to determine the level of compatibility between two COBOL compilers, it is necessary to determine:

- The version of the language standard supported
- Which modules are implemented
- Which level of each module is provided
- Whether any nonstandard extensions have been included

While this determination may seem complex, COBOL has well-defined formal standards that can be used as the basis for comparison. For many other languages and DBMSs, there are no such guidelines, thereby complicating the determination of program compatibility.

## Dynamic or Static Migration

Program migration, in either object or source form, can be dynamic or static. In the dynamic mode, the program is moved when data access is requested. In the static mode, the need for program migration is recognized during system design, and a copy of the program is established at the desired location prior to the need for its use. Although the latter case might not be considered program migration, the result is the same.

**Dynamic Program Movement.** This movement involves sending the equivalent of a job to the remote computer for execution. If the program is sent in object form, the job consists of the object program (possibly prelinked and/or link edited), the required JCL, and any input data needed. If the program is sent in source form, the job consists of the source program with JCL requesting compilation followed by execution and input data.

Obviously, an extremely fast response cannot be expected in either program migration method. Dynamic program movement is best suited to specific situations. For example, dynamic program movement is useful when an expert programmer is using a terminal to browse through a distributed data base, preparing the programs needed for remote access as browsing progresses. The dynamic mode is also useful when large amounts of remote data are required to complete an unanticipated report. Therefore, in any situation that requires remote access to large volumes of data but does not require rapid response, dynamic program migration can be used.

**Static Program Migration.** This form of migration allows time for pre-planning because the program is moved and established at the remote location prior to its use. When access is actually required, only a program-initiation request and any needed input data are sent.

If fast response is needed, however, the static migration mode is more suitable than the dynamic mode. In both modes the differences between the computers involved must be fully explored.

### Secondary Data Migration

Even though the strategy chosen to provide access to remotely stored data is program migration, data migration often results. In Figure 9-4, the basic problem is to provide the user at terminal A1 with access to data base segment B. Presumably, the user will want some of the data obtained to be returned to terminal A1, thereby causing data movement. In addition, in order to determine which data elements are required from segment B, it will probably be necessary to send input data to the remote location. Thus, program migration problems as well as data migration problems must be solved by the system designer.

### DATA MIGRATION

Data migration depends on sending a data access (and possibly update) request to some program at the remote location that will perform the required operation and return the desired result. The program at the remote location may be an application routine written specifically for this purpose. This routine is called a surrogate process or server process. Alternatively, the remote program may be the DBMS if it can accept access requests from remote locations.

## Format and Structural Differences

When data elements are moved between unlike computers, the data must be meaningful to, and usable by, the receiving application or user. Translations may be needed to convert between unlike data formats, as well as to resolve differences in the structures of the two data base segments. The required translations can be very simple or extremely complex.

## Dynamic or Static Migration

Data migration, like program migration, can be either dynamic or static.

**Dynamic Data Migration.** This migration occurs at the time the access is requested and is most often used to obtain small amounts of remotely stored data. Online transaction processing or time-sharing users or programs are most likely to generate this type of request. Even when data migration requests and responses occur dynamically, the data movement must be preplanned. The necessary surrogate application or server DBMS must be established at the remote location and must be available to respond to data base access requests when received.

**Static Data Migration.** This migration can be used for access to a large volume of data. If it is known that a definable set of data elements will be accessed, the entire set of data can be moved to the location where the data is needed. The data can then be accessed, and if it has been updated, the revised version can be moved back to the original location.

Static data migration is shown in Figure 9-5. When payroll checks must be printed for office A, the pay records for that office are moved from the host processor to the satellite processor at office A. The paycheck application is run against that data set, producing the checks as output. In this case, since no updates have been performed, there is probably no need to return the data to headquarters. If, however, the data is updated, the data set can be returned to the host to replace the earlier data copy.

The key to successful static data migration is to avoid concurrent updating of the master copy of the data and the temporary copy at the remote location. Updating two or more copies of the same data concurrently causes a very complex data reconciliation problem for which there are no general solutions—these can only be formulated within the framework of the specific application.

Independent updating is manageable, however, if different fields or records are involved. For example, a remote copy of an inventory data base might be updated to reflect changes in current stock balances at the same time the master is being updated to reflect price changes. Reconciling the two versions then involves using descriptive information from the master and

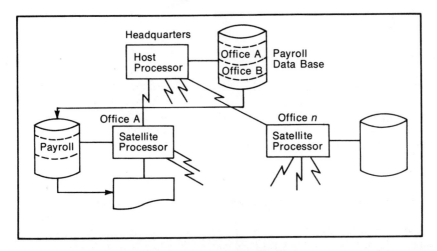

**Figure 9-5. Static Data Migration**

balance information from the copy. Data migration is clearly more complex if the remote access involves updating. To minimize complications, update during data migration should be avoided whenever possible.

## DATA FORMAT DIFFERENCES

Data migration between unlike computers almost always involves data conversion because of the differences between the respective computers' hardware and software. Program migration may also trigger data migration, again causing conversion.

Conversion routines must deal with data format differences as well as data base structural differences. Data formats can vary widely because of inherent differences in computer hardware or because of the software approaches chosen.

### Code Sets

The code sets used to store the segments of the distributed data base may be different. The most commonly used code sets for data storage are ASCII and EBCDIC. Some computer systems, however, use other codes, and even though two computers may both use the ASCII code set, for example, one may use a fuller set of the possible codes.

Converting data from one code set to another is basically a straightforward process, but provision must be made for handling characters or codes that occur in one set but not in the other. Some convention must be adopted for coping with these unmappable codes.

If unmappable codes do not require conversion, they can be translated into space or null characters. Occasionally, for example, printer-control codes are carried in stored data for quick output to hard-copy devices. Because these types of codes are device specific, they do not have to be translated when moving the data to another computer system. If unmappable codes must be carried, each code can be converted to a 2-character sequence in the target code set. The first of the two codes is an "escape" or "flag" character, and the second indicates which unmappable code is represented. This flexible approach allows a larger code set to be mapped to a smaller code set, without any data loss.

## Word, Field, or Record Size

Data movement may also be affected by differences in the word, field, and/or record sizes on each computer. As in the case of code sets, the difficulty arises when one computer has a larger maximum size than the other.

Word- and field-size differences are usually a problem when binary data is stored. A binary field may be limited to one or two computer words in length (e.g., 32 or 64 bits in a computer whose word size is 32 bits). The movement of binary data can therefore pose a problem. For example, in moving binary data from a 36-bit-word-size computer to a 32-bit machine, either data precision may be lost or the data must be expanded to 64 bits for storage.

If this situation exists in a distributed data base, three methods are possible for handling the binary data. First, all data can be carried in character or packed decimal form rather than binary. This approach, however, can waste storage space and cause conversions to/from binary when the data must be used in calculations. Second, extra space can be allocated in the smaller computer to accommodate the data from the larger computer. In the case of variable-length byte-size fields, this is the best approach. If binary data must be stored in full-word increments, however, this method wastes storage space. Finally, the computer that supports a larger word, field, or record can be arbitrarily constrained to support the same size as the other computer. Although this may waste some storage capacity of the larger computer, it may avoid complex translations and/or wasteful space use on the smaller computer. In the total system context, therefore, this may be the best choice.

All of these format differences—code set, word size, field size, and record length—can be handled quite easily. If the data base formats used in each segment of the distributed data base are fully documented, mapping or conversion routines can be easily devised for data translation.

If the distributed data base is in the process of being designed, there is considerable flexibility in constructing formats that require minimal conversion. For example, as noted earlier, in the case of two different word sizes, it may be most efficient to use only part of the capability of the larger computer, thereby ensuring compatibility with the smaller one. If, however, the distributed data base is being formed from two existing separate data bases that are independently designed, there is less flexibility in constructing formats. The problems of accommodation, therefore, will be more complex.

## STRUCTURAL DIFFERENCES

While differences in data formats are easy to manage, a distributed data base established on unlike computers can also involve structural differences. These differences are typically more difficult to handle.

### Structures and Access Methods

Structural differences involve the interrecord data relationships of the data base. For example, in an indexed-sequential structure, the records are stored semisequentially and accessed through one or more indexes. Access methods for this structure involve requesting a record through its identifying field(s). The DBMS then uses the indexes as necessary to obtain the requested record, which is then passed to the requesting program (and perhaps through that program to a terminal user).

Another implementation of an indexed structure might use a different number of indexes and/or might physically place records on the storage medium using a different storage strategy. Nevertheless, the same access request could be fulfilled in this second implementation, without the differences being apparent to a terminal user or to the application program developer.

There are, however, structural differences that are difficult to map. For example, the CODASYL model of data storage assumes that the user or programmer is a "navigator" [3] moving through the data base, seeking specific items of interest.

Figure 9-6 shows a network data structure consistent with the CODASYL data model. In this structure, logically related records are associated into sets. For each set, one type of record is the set owner, and one or more other record types are set members. For example, in a customer-order data base, each

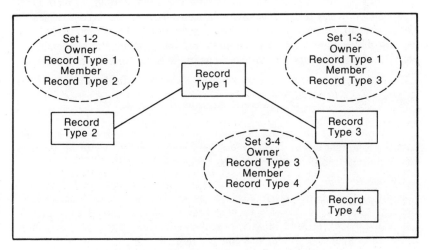

**Figure 9-6. CODASYL Data Base Structure**

customer record might be the owner of a set, while order records are members of the set. To obtain data from this type of network data structure, the programmer writes such statements as FIND NEXT RECORD-NAME WITHIN SET-NAME, FIND PRIOR RECORD-NAME WITHIN SET-NAME, and so on. These access requests are linked to the data model used—in this case, a network consisting of owner/member record sets. Thus, it is somewhat difficult to map these same access requests onto a different structure; attempting to execute a FIND NEXT RECORD-NAME WITHIN SET-NAME command against an indexed-sequential structure is meaningless since the data structure model does not include the concept of sets.

Structural differences cause difficulty because of the desirability of providing common access methods, despite the use of different structures. This is true regardless of whether the access strategy chosen is to migrate the data or the program.

## Structure-Independent Access Methods

As might be expected, access methods that are independent of the data structure are most easily mapped to different structures. The trade-off, however, is that these methods may also be relatively costly in terms of the computer resources used.

Approaches most often encountered with relational data bases [4] tend to be very structure independent. LINUS (Logical Inquiry and Update System) software, available for use with Honeywell's Multics Relational Data Store, allows the user to formulate such queries as SELECT NUMBER FROM PHONE BOOK WHERE NAME = "SMITH JOHN C." With this type of access method, the user formulating the query need have no knowledge of the data base except that it contains certain data elements. How these elements are stored and any interelement relationships need not be apparent to the user.

It is theoretically possible to map a structure-independent access request to many different structures. The efficiency and response speed achieved depend on both the complexity of the mapping and the particular implementation. Because of these factors, performance can range from excellent to unacceptable.

## Mapping Structure-Dependent Access Methods

Structure-dependent access requests can be mapped onto a data structure different than that envisioned in the access request. One way to accomplish this is through multilevel mapping, as shown in Figure 9-7.

By choosing a conceptual or reference data model (perhaps a relational structure, although not all researchers agree that this is the correct data model), it should be possible to map any actual data model to/from that conceptual model. It should also be possible to map any type of access request to the conceptual data model and thus to any real data structure. Although a very neat diagram of this approach can be drawn, its practicality remains to be

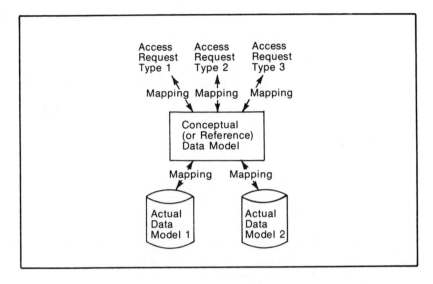

**Figure 9-7. Mapping Data Models and Access Requests**

proven. Even if logical feasibility is established, it may be difficult to provide an implementation with acceptable performance and response. Realistically, such a general mapping currently belongs to the realm of theory rather than of practice. In mapping access requests onto different structures, the most practical approach today is to use a structure-independent access method similar to LINUS or "Query by Example" (QBE)[5]. Although these are relatively easy to translate to different structures, doing so while providing an adequately fast response can present a challenge.

## DISTRIBUTED DATA BASE TRANSPARENCY

As noted earlier, data format and/or structure conversion will be necessary in most cases where a distributed data base is established on unlike computers, regardless of whether program or data migration is used to access remote data elements.

Where the necessary conversion takes place has a considerable impact on application and user independence from the distributed data base. This concept of independence is called transparency. If the requesting application program or terminal user must perform the data or structural conversions, data base changes can affect the program or user. In addition, the procedures for data base access can be more cumbersome and inconvenient for (presumably) multiple users and/or programs.

It is more advantageous to perform the conversion in the server application or DBMS, if possible. This centralizes the conversion routines so that if changes are required, only one set of software is affected. The conversion process will also be transparent to the terminal users or application programs.

Transparency is also affected by how the required data elements are located within the distributed data base. If the application program or terminal user must manually determine where elements are located, transparency is low, and any movement of data will affect people and programs. If data elements are located by the system through the use of global schemata and/or global catalogs, transparency is improved.

## CONCLUSION

Providing access for users and applications at the different computers to the various segments of the distributed data base requires careful planning so that the differences involved do not make data base access unacceptably difficult. The choice between program and data migration should be based on minimizing transmission volume (and therefore cost). The different possibilities must be analyzed in the context of the specific application, and the one that requires the lowest volume of data transmission should be chosen.

If program migration is selected, program differences must be resolved. If data migration is chosen, data format and/or structural differences must be resolved. Often both types of differences must, in practice, be handled, regardless of which strategy is chosen.

Straightforward translation methods are adequate to resolve data differences. Differences in data base structures, however, are more complex to handle. While some elegant theoretical approaches can be considered, in practice, remote access between radically different data structures is quite difficult to achieve. Rather than considering a generic ''ideal'' solution, a translation method that can handle the specific structures involved should be used.

Since ease of use and flexibility for change are important aspects of any distributed system, transparency should be an objective in every distributed data base implementation.

References

1. Booth, G.M. "Distributed Data Bases in Distributed Processing." *Infotech State of the Art Report*, Vol. 2 Maidenhead UK: Infotech International Ltd. 1977.
2. Booth, G.M. "Distributed Information Systems." *Proceedings of the 1976 National Computer Conference*, Montvale NJ.
3. Bachman, C.W. "The Programmer as Navigator." Turing Lecture in *CACM*, Vol. 16, No. 11 (November 1973), 653–658.
4. Codd, E.F. "A Relational Model of Data for Large Shared Data Banks." *CACM*, Vol. 13, No. 6 (June 1970), 377–387.
5. Zloof, M.M. "Query-By-Example—Operations on Hierarchical Data Bases." *Proceedings of the 1976 National Computer Conference*, Montvale NJ.

# ⑩ IMS/VS Implementation Case Study

by Myles E. Walsh

## INTRODUCTION

This case study involves the implementation of IMS/VS at a large, centralized data center. The data center is a corporate facility that processes computerized applications of several divisions of a $4 billion per year corporation. In the spring of 1980, the equipment configuration of the data center included three large-scale IBM computers, more than 180 spindles of direct-access storage (DASD), approximately 30 magnetic tape drives, and a magnetic tape library containing nearly 30,000 reels of tape. The facility supported a telecommunications network of more than 250 lines with 1,800 terminals of various types connected to them. The data center was processing about 250,000 transactions a day against the online files and data bases and was turning around approximately 120,000 batch jobs per month. These configuration and production statistics include the equipment requirements and the activity of the applications using the data base management system. The DP environment had not always been like this.

In 1976, when the corporate data processing department decided to investigate data base management, the data center housed computers that had only 25 percent of the computing power of the 1980 configurations and less than one-half of the DASDs. Online transaction volumes were also less than one-half: there were 150 telecommunications lines and about 800 terminals. Concurrent with the plunge into data base management was a commitment on the part of corporate DP to increased computer processing capabilities via virtual storage technology, time sharing for applications development, and computer networking.

The divisional DP director, committed to developing an application that would use a data base and the DBMS, began the design and development work simultaneously with the corporate study on the various DBMS products. By the time the corporate study was completed, the overall design work was also almost completed, and a significant portion of the elements that were to be included in the application's data base had been defined and documented (see Figure 10-1). The latter task had been assigned to an individual who had been appointed as the divisional data base administrator (DBA).

| Task | 1976 Winter | Spring | Summer | Fall | 1977 Winter | Spring | Summer | Fall | 1978 Winter | Spring | Summer | Fall | 1979 Winter | Spring | Summer | Fall | 1980 Winter | Spring |
|---|---|---|---|---|---|---|---|---|---|---|---|---|---|---|---|---|---|---|
| Decision to investigate DBMS Environment | ▮ | | | | | | | | | | | | | | | | | |
| Study group met | | ▬▬ | | | | | | | | | | | | | | | | |
| First application designed | | ▬▬ | | | | | | | | | | | | | | | | |
| IMS/VS support group established | | | ▮ | | | | | | | | | | | | | | | |
| First project team formed | | | ▮ | | | | | | | | | | | | | | | |
| Rudimentary IMS/VS batch processing system implemented | | | | ▬ | | | | | | | | | | | | | | |
| Online and data communications features implemented; DD/D became the first application to run online | | | | ▬ | | | | | | | | | | | | | | |
| Other divisions show interest; additional project teams set up for assistance | | | | | | ▮ | | | | | | | | | | | | |
| Accounts receivable application placed into production mode | | | | | | | | | ▮ | | | | | | | | | |
| Two small applications developed | | | | | | | | | | ▬▬ | | | | | | | | |
| New IMS/VS released and installed | | | | | | | | | | | ▮ | | | | | | | |
| Sample tracking system placed into production mode in test control region | | | | | | | | | | | ▮ | | | | | | | |
| Master catalog application placed into production mode | | | | | | | | | | | | | ▮ | | | | | |
| First large application placed into production mode | | | | | | | | | | | | | | ▮ | | | | |
| Another small application placed into production mode | | | | | | | | | | | | | | | ▮ | | | |

**Figure 10-1. Time Phases of the Project**

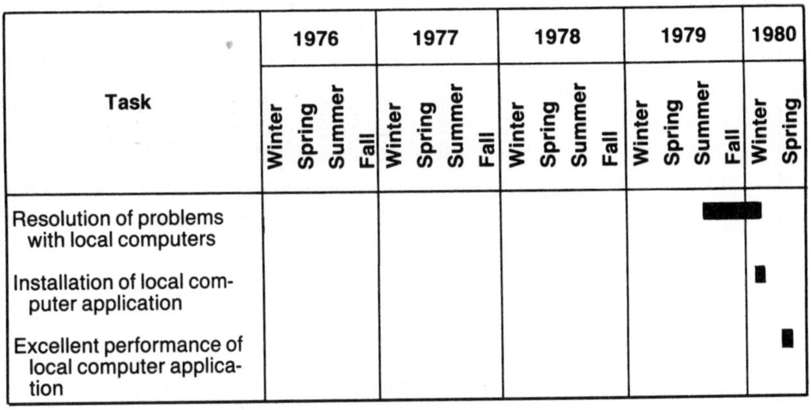

| Task | 1976 | | | | 1977 | | | | 1978 | | | | 1979 | | | | 1980 | |
|---|---|---|---|---|---|---|---|---|---|---|---|---|---|---|---|---|---|---|
| | Winter | Spring | Summer | Fall | Winter | Spring | Summer | Fall | Winter | Spring | Summer | Fall | Winter | Spring | Summer | Fall | Winter | Spring |
| Resolution of problems with local computers | | | | | | | | | | | | | | | ▬ | | | |
| Installation of local computer application | | | | | | | | | | | | | | | | | ▮ | |
| Excellent performance of local computer application | | | | | | | | | | | | | | | | | ▮ | |

**Figure 10-1. (Cont)**

At the time, the title data base administrator was quite fluid. It was used to describe everything from a corporate executive who was to be responsible for the corporation's data resource to a technical/clerical person who was to document data descriptions. The divisional DBA had, at this point, listed nearly every data element for the new application and the characteristics and attributes of each and had begun to define the relationships that existed among the elements. It was these relationships that would transform the collection of data elements into a divisional data base for the application.

The application itself had been segregated into two systems: an order entry, order inquiry, billing, and shipping system and an accounts receivable and cash application system. The two, although separate, had common interfaces on several of the files (i.e., some of the files were used by both systems). Each of the systems had an online and a batch facility. The online facilities were to be available 10 hours a day, from 8:00 A.M. until 6:00 P.M., and the batch facilities were to be run between 6:00 P.M. and 8:00 A.M. These parameters were established by September 1976, when the project team was formed.

Having selected the IMS/VS data base management system (DBMS) one month earlier, the corporate DP department formed an organization to support it. Two separate groups were set up. One was a systems software programming group that was responsible for the installation, support, enhancement, and troubleshooting of all data-base-related software products. The other group was a technical support group that was initially responsible for assisting divisions in data base design and reconciling the divisional data base requirements with the data center capacity. This latter aspect of the technical support group's responsibility required a high degree of both technical and political skill. The individuals in this group were also given the title of data base administrator. By September, the two groups consisted of two DBAs, a director of technical services, one systems software programmer, and a director of data base systems. All five became part of a project team.

## The Project Team

The function of the project team was to periodically bring together those individuals involved with the details of the design, implementation, and operation of the application. Members of the project team included a nucleus of individuals who attended every meeting and several other individuals whose attendance was required from time to time. The nucleus included individuals representing the following functions:

- Divisional DBA
- Corporate DBA
- Systems programmer
- Applications project manager
- Auditor

Other functions from which representation was required frequently, but not always, included:

- Divisional DP director
- Director of technical services
- Director of data base systems
- Divisional operations supervisor
- Corporate operations supervisor
- Director of systems software
- Various application programmers
- IBM systems engineer

In addition to the project team, there was a steering committee consisting of individuals higher up in the divisional and corporate organizations. This committee included:

- Corporate vice president of DP
- Divisional DP director
- Various divisional directors (the management of those functions that were to use the system in its operational state)
- Corporate operations director

On some occasions, members of the project team would attend steering committee meetings, thereby maintaining communications between the two groups.

## THE PRELIMINARY STAGES

By the end of 1976, several project team meetings had been held, and a rudimentary IMS/VS batch processing system had been generated and was in use. It had been determined that several additional data-base-related software products were needed. The most pressing need was for a data dictionary system. Of secondary importance was the need for a product that would facilitate the testing of online transactions by simulation in a batch processing environment. Both products were ordered before the end of 1976. The simulator, an IBM product known as the Batch Terminal Simulator (BTS), was set up first, simply because it was easy to install. It was operational almost immediately. Implementing the data dictionary product was somewhat more complicated.

The need for a data dictionary was agreed upon by everyone involved with the project because the idea of someone trying to keep field, record, file, and data base information up to date and synchronized, with copies distributed to all individuals who needed them, was judged an impossible task. The suggestion of a centralized computer file containing all the required information, available on an inquiry basis, appealed to everyone.

Several products were evaluated, and the IBM data dictionary/directory (DD/D) was selected. It was then decided that the DD/D should become the first application to use the IMS/VS system within the data center environment, especially because it could serve as an ideal test vehicle for the online IMS/VS and the data communications facilities.

In April 1977, the online and data communications feature of IMS/VS was generated, and the DD/D became the first application to run online. The test was successful, and in less than a month it was possible to begin testing online transactions for the divisional applications.

During the remainder of 1977 and in early 1978, several significant factors became apparent:
- Separate test and production facilities were needed.
- Other divisions were interested in DBMS.
- Staffing needs were increasing.
- Training was going to be expensive.
- Interfacing with other software would add to the complexity of required support.

After the online facilities testing began, it became apparent that testing and production could not be run on the same system. The architecture of the IMS/VS online feature is such that it has a single control region performing all I/O operations, while application transactions execute in separate regions, known as message-processing regions. An individual transaction is executed in a specific message-processing region, and the I/O activities of the transaction are channeled through the control region. In a testing environment, it is expected that some transactions will process erroneously and abnormally terminate (abend), creating extra work for the control region. Thus, production transactions, which are supposed to execute quickly, would be slowed if they were executing while a test transaction was abending. Because one of the data center's objectives was to provide an environment in which production transactions could execute quickly, it was determined that separate facilities would be required for testing and production. The result was a forecasted need for twice the amount of resources originally estimated.

In the spring of 1977, several other divisions began inquiring about the capabilities of data base management, in general, and IMS/VS in particular. To assist DP personnel in these divisions, project teams were set up similar to those established in the fall of 1976. The experience gained by those already involved was shared with those making the inquiries.

The inquiries were from divisions that had small applications in mind. For example, one division wanted to put a master catalog of its products, cross-referenced with other material, into a data base system. Another division wished to put up a sample tracking system using online IMS/VS facilities. Both of these applications involved relatively small files and a small volume of transactions. The project teams began initial analysis and design work.

It became apparent immediately that more people were needed in corporate technical services and in data base systems software support and that a significant amount of IMS/VS education was required, especially in the area of data base systems software. Therefore, two systems software specialists were added during 1977, and in early 1978, two DBAs were added on the corporate side.

At that time, the IMS/VS online and data communications facilities and the DD/D online feature were relatively new products. Consequently, no one was experienced in their use or support. It was necessary to train both the data base systems software specialists and the DBAs from the ground up. Divisional DBAs and application programming personnel also required training. It was estimated that training over a two-year period for corporate DP and four divisions could cost as much as $100,000. Since that time, IBM has dropped many of the courses and has replaced them with self-study programs that are somewhat less expensive. Table 10-1 contains a list of recommended courses, arranged by job (costs are subject to change). Other vendors have developed courses to fill the void left by IBM.

**Other Technologies.** IMS/VS and the DD/D were not the only complex technologies that had to be dealt with in this implementation. Virtual storage technology, more sophisticated computers, and a more complicated operating system were very much a part of this, as were computer networks and telecommunications.

The whole idea of access methods had also changed. Access methods such as BSAM, QSAM, BDAM, ISAM, and BTAM, which contain the program modules necessary to transfer data between peripheral devices and computer storage, were giving way to VSAM and VTAM. VSAM, although referred to as an access method, is actually a complete data management facility capable of cataloging and keeping statistics on data sets stored on direct-access storage devices. VTAM is a complete telecommunications network facility that can support computer-to-computer communications and multiple systems access for terminals throughout the network.

In addition, the need for master terminal operations (MTO) support was recognized. Another feature of the IMS/VS online data communications facility is the master terminal. This function acts as IMS/VS system monitor, controller, and troubleshooter. Each IMS/VS data base requires a dedicated master terminal, with both a CRT terminal and a typewriter terminal. The typewriter records all messages in hard-copy form; the master terminal operator monitors and controls the system through the CRT terminal. The operator participates in the starting and stopping of telecommunications lines and terminals, displays system status, participates in recovery and restart operations, and is the focal point for responding to user questions in a production

Table 10-1. Training Courses for IMS/VS Implementation

| Course | Cost $ | Managers | Systems Software Technicians | DBAs | Application Programmers | Operations Personnel |
|---|---|---|---|---|---|---|
| James Martin Seminar | 1,150 | X | | | | |
| Data Base Design and Administration | 700 | X | | | | |
| Leo Cohen Seminar | 850 | X | X | X | X | X |
| IMS/VS Concepts and Facilities | 0 | X | X | | | |
| IMS/VS Functions for Application Programming | 410 | | | X | X | |
| *IMS/VS Data Base Implementation I | 869 | | X | X | | |
| *IMS/VS Data Base Implementation II | 1,000 | | X | X | | |
| IMS/VS Master Terminal Operations | 345 | X | X | | | X |
| IMS/VS Data Base Performance and Tuning | 1,105 | | X | X | | |
| IMS/VS Data Communications Implementation | 1,530 | | X | X | | |
| *DL/I Application Programming | 1,806 | | X | X | X | |
| *IMS/VS DC Application Programming | 500 | | X | X | X | |
| *IMS/VS Message Format Service | 325 | | X | | | |
| IMS/VS DC Performance Analysis | 902 | | X | | | |
| *IMS/VS Systems Control | 557 | | X | | | |
| IMS/VS—SNA Implementation | 775 | | X | | | |
| *VSAM Coding for OS/MVS | 357 | | X | | | |
| VSAM for Systems Programmers | 709 | | X | X | | |
| *DB/DC Data Dictionary | 571 | X | X | X | | |

* Self-study courses

environment. Concurrent with the recognition of the importance of this function came an awareness of another software product, Control IMS Realtime, from Boole and Babbage. It proved to be an extremely good investment because it provided a window into the IMS/VS online and data communications system.

### Application Installation

By early 1978, the IMS/VS system was fairly well established, and the first application, the accounts receivable and cash application system, was put into production. The original intention had been to put everything in together—order entry, billing, shipping, and so on—but not all of the components were ready. Special programs and procedures had to be created to compensate for the fact that the newly installed accounts receivable and cash application system had to interface with an existing non-IMS/VS system, rather than with the planned IMS/VS system, which also was not ready. After a few initial difficulties, however, the system ran quite well.

During the remainder of 1978, the two smaller systems that were being developed by the other divisions approached completion, and a new release of IMS/VS was generated and installed. In addition, the order entry, billing, and shipping application was postponed a few more times. Because of such delays, a peculiar situation began to develop.

When a problem is explained up the line in large organizations, there is a tendency for distortions to creep in. IMS/VS and data base management were starting to get a bad name; however, few of the reasons for the postponements had anything to do with data base technology or IMS/VS. The problems were those of magnitude; the proposed system was very large, both in terms of transaction volume and file size. In addition, it became clear that the application would require more than 24 hours to complete its daily processing cycle whenever a significant problem occurred. Basically, the application had an online requirement of 10 hours a day, 8:00 A.M. to 6:00 P.M., and a batch requirement of 7 or 8 more hours. When the online portion of the system was brought down in the evening, it was necessary to spend approximately four hours in IMS/VS housekeeping, backing up data bases, consolidating log files, and preparing performance statistics. Because these tasks required a total of 21 to 22 hours, only 2 hours were left to handle recovery and restart in the event of problems. This led to what could be called an interesting political climate.

In 1978, one of the key data base software technicians resigned to take a better position outside the company. This was the first turnover on the corporate side since the two groups had been established. (There was no further turnover until the spring of 1980, when another data base software technician was given a better position within another division of the company.) The resigning individual was replaced by the second in command within the group, and two more technicians were recruited from within the company, bringing the data base systems software support complement to four: a manager and three systems software technicians. The corporate technical services group had also added two more technicians, so now there were four DBAs.

The previously mentioned sample tracking system was put into production in December 1978. This was the first system having a user located in another city. The single biggest difficulty with this system's installation had been the number of groups working on it. In addition to technical services and data base system software, there were two application development teams that participated in its implementation. The user division had a team involved, and so did corporate DP. A few misunderstandings about who was to do what occurred, and some premature commitments were made to the user. Based on these commitments, the user cut over to production in October. In doing so, the user had burned his bridges, so there was no going back. This system ran "in production" from the user's point of view in the IMS/VS test control region. This also caused political friction. By December, however, the misunderstandings were overcome, and the application went into normal production. It processed between 10,000 and 15,000 transactions a day and had a small batch processing cycle that ran overnight. Aside from the typical telecommunications problems that occasionally occur in applications using interstate communications facilities, the application was trouble free.

In March 1979, the other division's master catalog application went into production. The problems with that system were minimal and primarily related to the user's lack of experience in data base and data communications technology. Once those hurdles were cleared, the system functioned quite well.

## Another Major Thrust

By the spring of 1979, then, there were four small- to moderate-sized IMS/VS applications in production: the DD/D, the accounts receivable/cash application system, the sample tracking system, and the master catalog system. After a couple of postponements, the large order entry, billing, and shipping system was being primed for another attempt at production in May 1979. At the same time, still another division was preparing applications for production.

In 1978, this fourth division had made some preliminary investigations into data base technology and IMS/VS and subsequently had made major commitments to use it. The commitments involved planning, data gathering, pilot application development, and major application development. The division reorganized its DP department and hired a number of new people. Planning was begun, data gathering commenced, and the pilot application was started. Several smaller applications were scheduled to begin after the planning and data gathering were completed. The major application was contracted to IBM for design, development, and implementation.

One of the small applications—a client, product, production, and shipping-status system—is essentially an inquiry system. The data bases are rather small and transaction volume low. The one new difficulty with this system was the introduction of distributed intelligence. When originally conceived, the application was somewhat larger; thus, a decision was made to implement it in stages.

Terminals using the application were to be located in four sites around the country. These terminals were to be part of a local computer configuration, which, in turn, would communicate to the host in the centrally located data center. Support for these local computers was to be the responsibility of the division; however, it was not that simple.

Specific software products were required in the data center's host computer to support the local computers. At the time, no one at the data center had experience with, or even the most basic training in, support of these devices. Most of the problems associated with the implementation of this application revolved around lack of experience in this area. As time passed, knowledge was gained, but it was a slow and sometimes painful process. It is to the credit of the project manager that, with all these difficulties, the delay in the installation schedule was less than two months. This application went into production in June 1979.

Thus, by June 1979, there were five IMS/VS applications in production, six project teams were meeting, and a seventh was about to be formed because another division expressed interest in IMS/VS. There were project teams for:
- The order entry, billing, and shipping application
- The client, product, production, and shipping status application
- A forecasting application, building on the master catalog application
- A financial commitments and disbursements application
- A second accounts receivable/cash application system for another division, using much of the first division's system
- A marketing data base system
- A circulation revenue information system

Of these, the marketing data base system represented the most significant development (except for the order entry, billing, and shipping application, which had been postponed again and rescheduled for October 1979). This system was scheduled for partial implementation in late summer, 1980.

During the spring of 1979, both data base system software and technical services added one staff member. There were then five DBAs and five systems software programmers. Of the systems software programmers, one was a manager.

By late summer of 1979, technical services, data base software, and other technical support functions at the data center were spending an inordinate amount of time attempting to resolve problems concerning the local computers used in the client, product, production, and shipping-status system. Attempting to identify the source of the problem was a frustrating part of the problem-solving effort. Technicians from different disciplines are often too busy with problems that have already been defined to collaborate in isolating a problem that may be someone else's.

The autumn of 1979 was a time of tremendous activity because the postponed order entry, billing, and shipping system was readied for implementation. Procedures were developed for the conversion, for the production system, and for Plan B, the procedure for going back to the old system if the new system malfunctioned. After a week of day and night activity, however, the system did not work. The online data communications portion of the system worked reasonably well, but several batch programs did not, and there was not enough time in the day to finish the cycle. Plan B went into effect, and the existing system was reactivated. After frustration levels began to decline, a new target date was set for late January 1980.

In situations such as the one just described, a certain amount of animosity builds up at all levels of an organization; a we/they mentality can develop. November and December 1979 were spent regrouping and getting ready for the January target date. Tempers subsided, and recriminations and accusations died down. This situation had become so tense that cooperation between divisional and corporate personnel was superficial and rather grudgingly achieved. Because of the tension, hard work, long hours, second guessing, and misunderstandings, individuals on each side were working in survival mode.

In January 1980, however, a second attempt worked. It took all of February and most of March for the system to settle down, but it eventually did. By June 1980, it was actually performing better in some respects than had originally been anticipated.

## WHAT WAS LEARNED

In the four years since data base and data base management systems were proposed, experience has provided some important insights. The project has also shown that some of the concerns about data base technology receive far too much attention at the expense of other important issues.

**Planning Considerations.** There is a great deal of discussion and literature dealing with the relative merits of data bases, hierarchical structures, and networks. Much of this is esoteric and primarily for the enlightenment of those who can understand it; it actually has little significance in the real-world situations in which DBMSs are found. Other factors, however, are of greater significance.

The advantages of one DBMS over another is another subject that is terribly overworked. The applications for the proposed DBMS and the operating environment into which it must be integrated, for example, represent two much more important considerations in selecting a DBMS. Discussing the relative merits of TOTAL, IMS/VS, SYSTEM 2000, and IDMS, without having a particular application in mind, is somewhat like discussing the relative athletic capabilities of Reggie Jackson, Johnny Bench, Steve Carlton, and Pete Rose. All are recognized and proven, but the application to which they are assigned is an important evaluation factor.

**Staffing and Training.** Once IMS/VS had been selected as the appropriate DBMS, the first concern was that of staffing. Skilled people of three types were needed: systems software technicians, file and data base designers, and application programmers. The latter, as it turned out, required less training than anticipated and were productive within a couple of months. An IMS/VS Concepts and Facilities course, a three-day course called Application Programming in an IMS/VS DB Environment, a two-day course called Application Programming in an IMS/VS DC environment, and another two-day course in IMS/VS Message Format Services (MFS) were all that were necessary for application programmer training. These four courses offered an overview of the concept and facilities of IMS/VS; illustrated how to write Data Language/I (DL/I) instructions that were integrated into PL/1, COBOL, or Assembler language programs; and taught how to prepare display formats for IBM 3270 CRT terminals. (DL/I, the IMS/VS I/O language, facilitates the transfer of data elements, called segments, between auxiliary storage devices and computer memory. MFS, a utility feature of IMS/VS, acts as an editor/ interface between messages appearing in application programs and displays appearing on terminal devices.) Within two months of taking these courses and after using what they had been taught, programmers were producing executable IMS/VS application programs.

The data base administrators and systems programmers eventually attended these courses, also. The DBAs took a few more courses initially and the system programmers took several more over an 18-month period so that training was accomplished both in the classroom and on the job. Members of both groups functioned on the job while they were learning. The courses taught the practical realities of using IMS/VS, the DD/D, and several other data base management productivity aids and support products and their integration into the daily data center operation. When individuals were added to the staffs, they received the same training as did their predecessors.

**Job Functions.** Sketchy job descriptions had been written initially but only because the personnel department required them so as to determine job levels and salaries. Over time, however, these jobs began to include specific functions. The application programmer job description was affected the least; it was modified slightly to require DL/I and MFS experience. Other job descriptions were completely rewritten. For example, the DBA function included experience in:
- DL/I and MFS
- File and data base design
- Data base definition (DBD)
- Program specification block (PSB)
- Data dictionary/directory (DD/D)
- Data base system standards
- Data base system product evaluation
- Generation of DBD and PSB control blocks
- Data base reorganization
- Interface between divisional and corporate personnel
- Data base design review

As the DBAs developed, they gained a wide range of technical and political skills.

The data base systems software technicians evolved into a highly valuable group of individuals. Their skills included:
- Data base system generations (GENS)
- Troubleshooting
- Supporting related data base system products
- Performance measuring and tuning
- Interfacing with data center operations
- Answering technical questions from various sources
- Assisting with application implementation
- Maintaining data base integrity (recovery and restart procedures)
- Assisting with data base reorganization
- Assisting with data base backup operations
- Enhancing data base systems software
- Handling the telecommunications software interface
- Handling the security software interface
- Handling the operating systems software interface

The corporate DBAs and the data base system software technicians serve in support roles. The DBA primarily functions in the design and development stages of a project; this role diminishes, however, as implementation approaches. The role of the system software technician, on the other hand, is minor during design and development; his or her involvement increases during implementation. Note that individuals from both groups belonged to the several project teams that were functioning during a given time interval.

**Standards.** Because a cooperative effort between the two groups was required, a set of internal data base and data dictionary standards was formulated. These standards were issued piecemeal but were ultimately published, about a year after IMS/VS was installed, as an internal standards manual. This manual is periodically modified; Table 10-2 shows the manual's table of contents.

**Installation.** DBAs and systems programmers had to address other situations that arose after the commitment to DBMS. These situations, which are described in the following paragraphs, are concerned with the installation of IMS/VS, the DD/D, and related products in the corporate data order described earlier.

Integrating a DBMS into an existing environment probably involves installing at least two generations: one for testing and development work, one for production. In organizations having multiple divisional users of the DBMS, more than two generations are needed if the existing resource billing system is unable to separate the various users.

As DBMS applications are developed, several sets of files or data bases may be needed (e.g., a complete set for the production systems, a separate

**Table 10-2. Standards Manual Table of Contents**

| Section | Description |
|---|---|
| 1. Naming Conventions | Complete naming convention requirements for all IMS applications. |
| 2. DL/I Programming Techniques | DL/I coding standards and guidelines for better performance of programs under IMS. |
| 3. IMS PL/1 Programming Techniques | PL/1 coding standards and guidelines to be used for all IMS PL/1 applications. |
| 4. MFS Standards/Guidelines | Message Formatting Services standards and guidelines required to efficiently map IMS messages with devices. |
| 5. Library Organization and Application Procedures | Complete list of test and production library names to be used for all IMS applications; IMS application PROCs for divisional use. |
| 6. User Application Code in IMS Control Region | Information about user-written routines for data base maintenance and available IMS data communications exits, as well as standards for using each feature. |
| 7. Broadcasting Messages and IMS System Commands for Divisional Use | Identification of broadcast messages and switches and a list of commands that can be entered by divisional users of IMS. |
| 8. DLIERROR | User documentation for the IMS Status Code Analyzer, DLIERROR, which must be included in all IMS programs developed in or for the organization. |
| 9. System Trouble Sheets | The Data Center System Trouble Sheet forms and instructions for reporting IMS computer system problems. |
| 10. System Resource and Transaction Security Forms | The data center forms and instructions needed to transmit system resources and transaction security requirements to the IMS software staff. |
| 11. Data Dictionary/Directory Standards | Forms and instructions designed for use by the systems/programming user or divisional DBA to define data to the DD/D. All IMS-related information to be defined must be entered into the DD/D. |
| 12. Glossary of Standard Abbreviations of Business Keywords for PL/1 Data Names | Construction of standard abbreviated keywords (commonly used business terms), along with standards and rules for constructing PL/1 data names for use in IMS applications. |
| 13. Sparse Index Routines and Customized Randomizer Routines | Divisional testing and implementation procedures for IMS Sparse Index routines, as well as customized IMS Randomizer routines. |
| 14. IMS Maintenance Procedures | Information concerning data dictionary updates, Division News Data Sets, ACBGEN schedules, IMS production maintenance checklist form, batch to online test steps, and online test to production steps. |
| 15. IMS Restart/Recovery | Applications requirements to take advantage of the IMS backup and recovery system. |
| 16. Unusual Abend Conditions and Inefficient Processing | Collection of unusual abend conditions encountered using IMS; also, inefficient processing techniques to avoid. |

subset for systems or volume testing, another subset for batch and unit testing). Careful attention should be given to direct-access storage device (DASD) estimates. Experience has shown that DASD requirements are often underestimated.

DBMSs in a data center environment either use or interface with the facilities of other software that is often equally if not more complex than the DBMS software itself. For example, in an IBM equipment configuration, interfaces must be established to such products as VSAM and VTAM. IMS/VS also uses the facilities of MVS (a sophisticated operating system). Some knowledge of each of these facilities is necessary for the DBAs and systems software technicians.

In addition to the support for the DBMS package itself, support is required for other related products. Included in this group is the already mentioned DD/D. There may also be a requirement for a report writer like MCAUTO's MRCS. Some users request any package that appears to facilitate their applications development work. Batch Terminal Simulator (BTS) is a package that tests online programs in a batch environment. IMSMAP is a productivity aid that produces graphic representations of logical data base schemas and subschemas. DB PROTOTYPE aids in testing various data base structures to evaluate alternatives. These are just a few of many.

Within IMS/VS-DC there is a feature known as the master terminal. A master terminal operator (MTO) who is, from an operations perspective, the owner/caretaker of the systems is required. This function is staffed with an individual who can respond to unexpected situations. This person must also act as the interpersonal communications interface for all IMS/VS users. The MTO is the first line of defense. When something goes wrong, the MTO is generally the first person on the corporate side to know about it, either through a message on the master terminal or a phone call from a user.

There are some aspects of IMS/VS where timing is very important. Although they seem almost too obvious to state, they are sometimes overlooked by overly optimistic application developers. Recoveries of large-scale data bases, for example, can be elaborate and time-consuming. The longest outage during the last four years was a recovery situation that took three days from the occurrence of the error to the point of restoring the data bases to usable condition. Although the system had indicated a probable error, it was decided to run a day's work online. When checked at end of day, it was found that a major data base had been damaged. Several hours were spent planning recovery, several more executing it, and several more checking the results. That was an extreme case, however; most recoveries are completed within minutes, while some take an hour or two.

Reorganization of a large-scale data base often takes several hours. In theory, reorganization should not be required often if data bases are designed properly. In practice, however, parameters change, users think of new ideas, and the data bases, as designed, are no longer adequate. Thus, reorganization should be anticipated. For applications requiring most of a 20-hour day to process, reorganizations must be scheduled on weekends.

Data bases must be backed up periodically. A dynamic data base, one that is updated frequently, should be backed up daily. Although this is time-consuming, it must be planned as part of the daily schedule. Waiting longer saves daily processing time, but the trade-off is that recovery, when needed, may be substantially longer and more complex.

People are not machines. Every attempt should be made to spread responsibilities for critical tasks among as many individuals as possible. Too much responsibility can cause individuals to make mistakes, become ill, or resign. Each of these consequences is undesirable.

## CONCLUSION

IMS/VS is a complex system, especially when run as a multiple-user system in a multiple-machine, multiple-user environment. Implementation time, amount of training, training costs, and so on often exceed original estimates.

Some generalizations can be gleaned from the experience of IMS/VS implementation. Speed of retrieval is traded for simplicity of function. Retrieval is quick, but file maintenance can be appreciably slower than with conventional files. Although data redundancy is reduced, processing complexity is increased (this is the old space/processing trade-off). Data independence, the isolation of data files from programs, creates more productive application programming and less complex maintenance of both files and programs. The primary trade-off, however, is the creation of a whole new technical specialization—data base administration—with a high price tag.